90-DAY OPTOMETRY PRACTICE PLANNER

BETTER VISION - BETTER LIFE - BETTER WORLD

DR. BRENDA MONTECALVO

BRIGHT INK PRESS

Hardcover ISBN: 978-1-965905-10-4

Published by Bright Ink Press
12 Boulevard, Tallapoosa, GA

WELCOME

01

Brenda Heinke Montecalvo, OD, FOVDR, FAAO, FCSO, is a passionate, sought-after international speaker. As a doctor of optometry, she specializes in vision therapy and helps students become successful in school. With a strong desire to change lives, Dr. Montecalvo uses her knowledge and ability to determine how students can be more efficient learners. She has provided primary care optometry to her patients in a successful private practice setting for over 38 years.

Dr. Montecalvo presents the annual Cedarville Seminar Series for Optometric Vision Therapy (OVT) to international audiences. She also lectures in the areas of Neuro-Optometric Rehabilitation (NOR), strabismus, amblyopia, OVT, prescribing of therapeutic performance lenses, preventive eye care, and Practice Management (PM).

She is the best-selling author of *Visual Secrets for School Success,* is co-author of the American Optometric Association (AOA) Brain Injury Electronic Resource Manual, and has authored several articles about NOR, OVT and Practice Management.

Dr. Montecalvo is a Fellow of the Optometric Vision Development and Rehabilitation Association, Fellow of the American Academy of Optometry, Fellow of the College of Syntonic Optometry, and has achieved Skill Level II in NORA. Dr. Montecalvo is Past Chair of the AOA Vision Rehabilitation Section (VRS) and is a member of the AOA InfantSEE Committee. She is Past President of the Ohio Optometric Association, Past President of the Neuro-Optometric Rehabilitation Association (NORA), is Co-Chair of the John Streff Invitational Lens Symposium, and is a trustee of the Vision Leads Foundation. She graduated with distinction from the Pacific University College of Optometry.

Dr. Montecalvo's interests include enjoying time with her three adult children and grandchildren, being active in her church, gardening, and operating a horse farm with her husband, Anthony.

YEARLY PLANNING 02

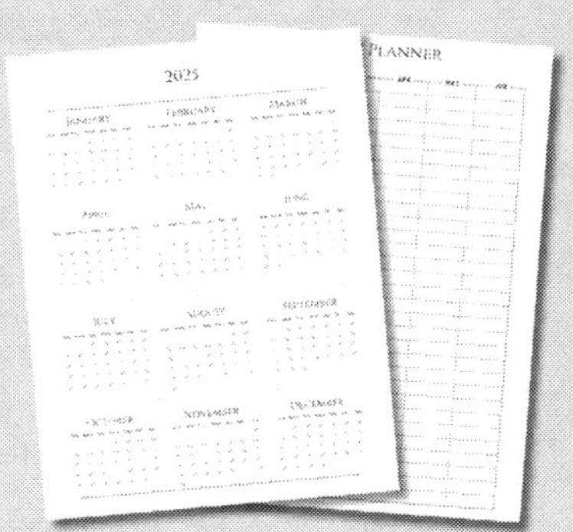

The yearly forms provide a clear-eyed look at upcoming events. They determine how far and how fast your practice can grow.

Utilize the yearly planning:

1. What big picture priorities does your practice want to accomplish?
(Examples: Marking off your vacations, launching a workshop, marketing events, and seminars)

2. What are the key seasons, events, or deadlines for which you need to pre-plan?
(Think: back-to-school rush, vision awareness month, annual conferences, staff trainings.)

3. What programs, promotions, or partnerships do you want to execute?
(Map out rough start dates, content or campaign themes, and roles.)

Tips for Using This Sheet:

- Highlight anchor months—months where a lot is happening and may need early prep.
- Block off pre-planning marketing campaigns and important content themes now so your team has time to create, schedule, and shine.
- Leave buffer time around holidays or personal time off—this will protect your team's energy.
- Revisit this sheet at the start of each month to adjust or recommit.

Quarterly Planning 03

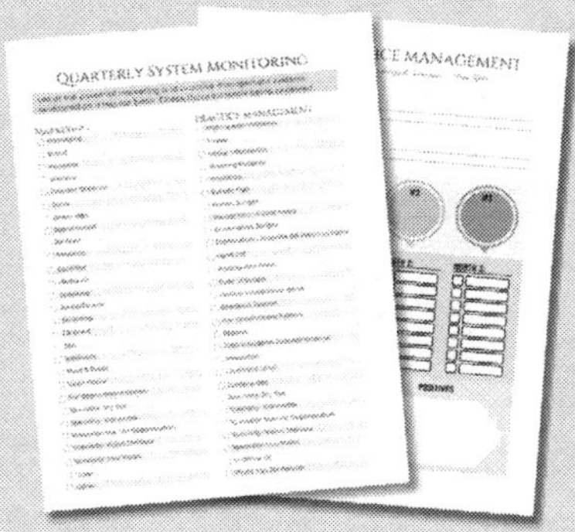

Use the QUARTERLY PRACTICE MANAGEMENT page to reconnect with your clinic's why and where you're headed. Revisit your mission and vision, are they still true? Do they inspire your team? Update language if needed.

Use the QUARTERLY SYSTEMS MANAGEMENT page to take inventory of what's actually running in your clinic by reviewing the systems and strategies listed. Check off what's currently being implemented and circle or star the ones you'd like to focus on this quarter.

This quick audit helps you stay consistent, identify gaps, and make strategic adjustments. Do this with your team at the start of the quarter for alignment and accountability.

Write out your core values to guide your decision-making this quarter. Then, set your:

- Short-term goals (achievable within this quarter)
- Long-term goals (visionary goals for the next 6–18 months)

Keep these goals visible during weekly meetings. Progress follows clarity.

MONTHLY PLANNING 04

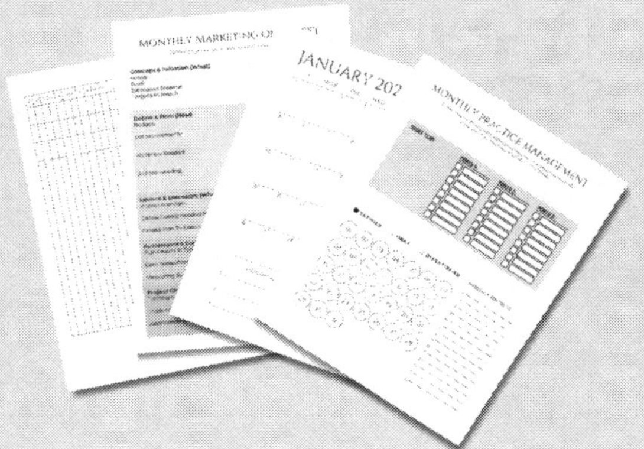

Practice management, marketing and benchmarks need to be tracked and reviewed often. These are the very tools my Vision Aces Clients use to support and streamline their practices.

I created a fillable electronic copy of the Monthly Benchmarks Tracking sheet as a gift. Simply scan the code and you will prompted to edit the template.

You will find these six sheets right after your month calendar page. Take time to fill them in and reassess yourself, your staff, and your clinic practice. Get in the habit of sharing this information with your team, making your team meetings more successful.

Monthly Calendar: For quick scheduling, access each month.
Monthly Practice Management: Keeping your team on track with high performance.
Monthly Marketing Management: Tracking and development of effective growth strategies.
Monthly Benchmarks Tracking: Allowing you to track monthly practice performance.

DAILY PLANNING 05

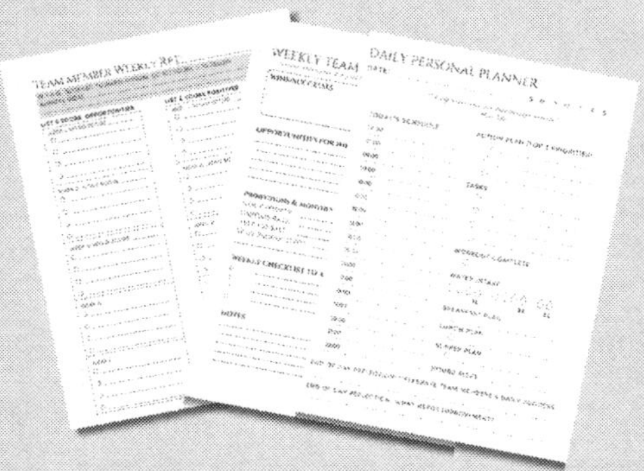

You will find these three forms work well for keeping your team and days on track.

Weekly Team Member Report: Each month include multiple copies of this form for listing, scoring, and ranking your team's opportunities and positives per team member.

Team Meeting: Use this team meeting template to streamline your weekly team meetings. You will find an area to log you and your team's positives, opportunities, and projects.

Daily Personal Planner: You will find 30 of these forms per month, prompting you to keep healthy and organized.

Free Resources

SO GLAD YOU ARE TAKING THE NEXT STEPS IN YOUR PRACTICE. LOOKING FORWARD TO CONNECTING!

2 HOURS TO GET A SUCCESSFUL <u>BUSINESS PLAN</u> THAT YOU CAN START USING IMMEDIATELY

- INCREASE PROFIT STRATEGIES: I'll go over the profit increasing strategies all practices need to be applying.
- TIME SAVING TIPS: I'll share 10 time-saving tips for you and your office.
- DEMONSTRATIONS: Learn the demonstrations that help your patients understand that they need better vision.
- CONVERT POTENTIAL VISION THERAPY PATIENTS INTO PAYING VISION THERAPY PATIENTS: Learn 3 of 10 ways to get your patients excited about joining your program.
- LEARNING DELAYS, STRABISMUS, AMBLYOPIA, BRAIN INJURY: Tips and tools to improve patient outcomes for all three.

2025

JANUARY

SUN	MON	TUES	WED	THUR	FRI	SAT
		01	02	03	04	05
06	07	08	09	10	11	12
13	14	15	16	17	18	19
20	21	22	23	24	25	26
27	28	29	30			

FEBRUARY

SUN	MON	TUES	WED	THUR	FRI	SAT
						01
02	03	04	05	06	07	08
09	10	11	12	13	14	15
16	17	18	19	20	21	22
23	24	25	26	27	28	

MARCH

SUN	MON	TUES	WED	THUR	FRI	SAT
						01
02	03	04	05	06	07	08
09	10	11	12	13	14	15
16	17	18	19	20	21	22
23	24	25	26	27	28	29
30	31					

APRIL

SUN	MON	TUES	WED	THUR	FRI	SAT
			01	02	03	04
05	07	07	08	09	10	11
12	13	14	15	16	17	18
19	20	21	22	23	24	25
26	27	28	29	30	31	

MAY

SUN	MON	TUES	WED	THUR	FRI	SAT
				01	02	03
04	05	06	07	08	09	10
11	12	13	14	15	16	17
18	19	20	21	22	23	24
25	26	27	28	29	30	31

JUNE

SUN	MON	TUES	WED	THUR	FRI	SAT
01	02	03	04	05	06	07
08	09	10	11	12	13	14
15	16	17	18	19	20	21
22	23	24	25	26	27	28
29	30					

JULY

SUN	MON	TUES	WED	THUR	FRI	SAT
		01	02	03	04	05
06	07	08	09	10	11	12
13	14	15	16	17	18	19
20	21	22	23	24	25	26
27	28	29	30	31		

AUGUST

SUN	MON	TUES	WED	THUR	FRI	SAT
					01	02
03	04	05	06	07	08	09
10	11	12	13	14	15	16
17	18	19	20	21	22	23
24	25	26	27	28	29	30
31						

SEPTEMBER

SUN	MON	TUES	WED	THUR	FRI	SAT
	01	02	03	04	05	06
07	08	09	10	11	12	13
14	15	16	17	18	19	20
21	22	23	24	25	26	27
28	29	30				

OCTOBER

SUN	MON	TUES	WED	THUR	FRI	SAT
			01	02	03	04
05	07	07	08	09	10	11
12	13	14	15	16	17	18
19	20	21	22	23	24	25
26	27	28	29	30	31	

NOVEMBER

SUN	MON	TUES	WED	THUR	FRI	SAT
						01
02	03	04	05	06	07	08
09	10	11	12	13	14	15
16	17	18	19	20	21	22
23	24	25	26	27	28	29
30						

DECEMBER

SUN	MON	TUES	WED	THUR	FRI	SAT
	01	02	03	04	05	06
07	08	09	10	11	12	13
14	15	16	17	18	19	20
21	22	23	24	25	26	27
28	29	30	31			

2026

JANUARY

SUN	MON	TUES	WED	THUR	FRI	SAT
				01	02	03
04	05	06	07	08	09	10
11	12	13	14	15	16	17
18	19	20	21	22	23	24
25	26	27	28	29	30	31

FEBRUARY

SUN	MON	TUES	WED	THUR	FRI	SAT
01	02	03	04	05	06	07
08	09	10	11	12	13	14
15	16	17	18	19	20	21
22	23	24	25	26	27	28

MARCH

SUN	MON	TUES	WED	THUR	FRI	SAT
01	02	03	04	05	06	07
08	09	10	11	12	13	14
15	16	17	18	19	20	21
22	23	24	25	26	27	28
29	30	31				

APRIL

SUN	MON	TUES	WED	THUR	FRI	SAT
			01	02	03	04
05	07	07	08	09	10	11
12	13	14	15	16	17	18
19	20	21	22	23	24	25
26	27	28	29	30	31	

MAY

SUN	MON	TUES	WED	THUR	FRI	SAT
					01	02
03	04	05	06	07	08	09
10	11	12	13	14	15	16
17	18	19	20	21	22	23
24	25	26	27	28	29	30
31						

JUNE

SUN	MON	TUES	WED	THUR	FRI	SAT
	01	02	03	04	05	06
07	08	09	10	11	12	13
14	15	16	17	18	19	20
21	22	23	24	25	26	27
28						

JULY

SUN	MON	TUES	WED	THUR	FRI	SAT
			01	02	03	04
05	07	07	08	09	10	11
12	13	14	15	16	17	18
19	20	21	22	23	24	25
26	27	28	29	30	31	

AUGUST

SUN	MON	TUES	WED	THUR	FRI	SAT
						01
02	03	04	05	06	07	08
09	10	11	12	13	14	15
16	17	18	19	20	21	22
23	24	25	26	27	28	29
30	31					

SEPTEMBER

SUN	MON	TUES	WED	THUR	FRI	SAT
		01	02	03	04	05
06	07	08	09	10	11	12
13	14	15	16	17	18	19
20	21	22	23	24	25	26
27	28	29	30			

OCTOBER

SUN	MON	TUES	WED	THUR	FRI	SAT
				01	02	03
04	05	06	07	08	09	10
11	12	13	14	15	16	17
18	19	20	21	22	23	24
25	26	27	28	29	30	31

NOVEMBER

SUN	MON	TUES	WED	THUR	FRI	SAT
		01	02	03	04	05
06	07	08	09	10	11	12
13	14	15	16	17	18	19
20	21	22	23	24	25	26
27	28	29	30	31		

DECEMBER

SUN	MON	TUES	WED	THUR	FRI	SAT
		01	02	03	04	05
06	07	08	09	10	11	12
13	14	15	16	17	18	19
20	21	22	23	24	25	26
27	28	29	30	31		

YEARLY PLANNER

	JANUARY	FEBRUARY	MARCH	APRIL	MAY	JUNE
01						
02						
03						
04						
05						
06						
07						
08						
09						
10						
11						
12						
13						
14						
15						
16						
17						
18						
19						
20						
21						
22						
23						
24						
25						
26						
27						
28						
29						
30						
31						

YEARLY PLANNER

	JULY	AUGUST	SEPTEMBER	OCTOBER	NOVEMBER	DECEMBER
01						
02						
03						
04						
05						
06						
07						
08						
09						
10						
11						
12						
13						
14						
15						
16						
17						
18						
19						
20						
21						
22						
23						
24						
25						
26						
27						
28						
29						
30						
31						

Quarterly Practice Management

Vision:

Mission:

CORE VALUES

SHORT TERM

MONTH 1:

MONTH 2:

MONTH 3:

LONG TERM

Quarterly System Management

List of the potential marketing and practice management systems monitored on a regular basis.
Check those currently being implemented.

Marketing:

- ☐ Messaging
- ☐ Brand
- ☐ Personas
- ☐ Website
- ☐ Content Creation
- ☐ Email
- ☐ Direct Mail
- ☐ Social Media
- ☐ Reviews
- ☐ Referrals
- ☐ Media Kit
- ☐ Speaking
- ☐ Radio/TV Ads
- ☐ Exhibiting
- ☐ CE Event
- ☐ SEO
- ☐ Webinars
- ☐ Meet & Greet
- ☐ Open House
- ☐ Expertise
- ☐ Pre-appointment System
- ☐ Specialty: Dry Eye
- ☐ Specialty: Glaucoma
- ☐ Specialty: Macular Degeneration
- ☐ Specialty: Vision Therapy
- ☐ Specialty: Low Vision
- ☐ Other:
- ☐ Other:

Practice Management

- ☐ Making Appointments
- ☐ Triage
- ☐ Intake Information
- ☐ Greeting Patients
- ☐ Insurance
- ☐ Benefit Plan
- ☐ Pretest Scripts
- ☐ Pretest Educational Items
- ☐ Examination Scripts
- ☐ Examination Chairside Educational Items
- ☐ Routing Info Sheet
- ☐ Optical Scripts
- ☐ Optical Educational Items
- ☐ Checkout System
- ☐ Pre-appointment System
- ☐ Reports
- ☐ Staff Education Internal/External
- ☐ Newsletter
- ☐ Communication
- ☐ Hand Off
- ☐ Conferences
- ☐ Specialty: Dry Eye
- ☐ Specialty: Glaucoma
- ☐ Specialty: Macular Degeneration
- ☐ Specialty: Vision Therapy
- ☐ Specialty: Low Vision
- ☐ In Office CE
- ☐ Thank You for Referral

MONTH:

SUN	MON	TUES	WED	THUR	FRI	SAT

MONTH GOALS

1. ______________________________

2. ______________________________

3. ______________________________

TO DO LIST

- ▢
- ▢
- ▢
- ▢
- ▢

Monthly Practice Management

SHORT TERM **MONTH 1:** **MONTH 2:** **MONTH 3:**

● Satisfied ⊘ Okay ⊗ Dissatisfied

Monthly Findings

1	2	3	4	5	6	7
8	9	10	11	12	13	14
15	16	17	18	19	20	21
22	23	24	25	26	27	28
29	30	31				

Monthly Marketing One-Sheet

"By Failing to prepare, you are preparing to fail." –Benjamin Franklin

Concept & Initiation (What)
Name:
Goal:
Estimated Timeline:
Targets to Reach:

Define & Plan: (How)
Budget:

List requirements:

Materials Needed:

Actions Needed:

Launch & Execution: (Who, When & Where)
Project Manager:

Define Details needed for each action:

Create Plan To Execute:

Performance & Control
Plan Details in Timeline:

Communication Plan Used:

Measuring Success:

Project Close
Training Needed:

Implementation Process:

Assessment of Success

Benchmarks: Professional

	Production YTD	Collections YTD	Net
Week 1			
Week 2			
Week 3			
Week 4			
Week 5			

KEY
YTD: Year to Date
M: Month
Ins. Coll: Insurance Collections
PT. Coll: Patient Collections
NP EX.: New Patient Exams
EP EX.: Established Patient
Exams
Total EX.: Total Exams
Prod. EX.: Production Per Exam
Coll. EX.: Collection Per Exam
Prof. Fees: Professional Fees

M	Ins. Coll.	Pt. Coll.	NP Ex.	EP Ex.	Total Ex.	Pro/ Ex.	Coll/ Ex.	Prof. Fees	Other	Other	Other
1											
2											
3											
4											
5											
6											
7											
8											
9											
10											
11											
12											

BENCHMARKS: RETAIL

	PRODUCTION YTD	COLLECTIONS YTD	NET
WEEK 1			
WEEK 2			
WEEK 3			
WEEK 4			
WEEK 5			

KEY
YTD: Year to Date
M: Month
Ins. Coll: Insurance Collections
PT. Coll: Patient Collections
# of Frames: Number of Frames
Fr. Coll.: Frames Collected
Ave Fr Sale: Average Frame Sale
Lens Sold: Number of Lens Sold
Fr. Coll.: Frames Collected
Ave. Lens Sale: Average Lens Sale
Cap. Rate: Capture Rate
CL Fit Eval: Total Contact Lens Fits
CL Yr Supp: Contact Lens Year Supply
CL Capt. Rate: Contact Lens Capture Rate
CL Coll: Contact Lens Collections
CL$/Fit: Average Contact Lens Sale/Fitting

M	INS. COLL.	PT. COLL.	# OF FRAMES	FR COLL.	AVE FR SALE	# LENS SOLD	FR COLL	AVE LENS SALE	CAP. RATE	CL FIT/ EVAL	CL YR SUPP	CL CAPT RATE	CL COLL	CL$ /FIT
1														
2														
3														
4														
5														
6														
7														
8														
9														
10														
11														
12														

Benchmarks: Special

	Production YTD	Collections YTD	Net
Week 1			
Week 2			
Week 3			
Week 4			
Week 5			

KEY
YTD: Year to Date
M: Month
Ins. Coll: Insurance Collections
PT. Coll: Patient Collections
VT Eval: Vision Therapy Evaluations
VT Conf: Vision Therapy Conferences
VT Sign-ups: Vision Therapy Sign-up
VT NS Rate: Vision Therapy No-show Rate
DE Eval: Vision Therapy Evaluations
DE Conf: Vision Therapy Conferences
DE Sign-ups: Vision Therapy Sign-up
CL Fit
CL Start: Contact Lens Starts
MD Eval: Macular Degeneration Evaluation
GL Eval: Glaucoma Evaluation
LV Eval: Low Vision Evaluation

M	Ins. Coll.	Pt. Coll.	VT Evals	VT Conf	VT Start	VT NS Rate	DE Eval	DE Conf	DE Start	CL Eval	MD Eval	GL Eval	LV Eval	Other
1														
2														
3														
4														
5														
6														
7														
8														
9														
10														
11														
12														

Benchmarks

Income

Income 1	
Income 2	
Other Income	
Total	

Expenses

Month

Budget

To be paid	Due Date	Amount	Paid	Notes

Summary

Total Income	Total Expenses	Difference

Notes

WEEKLY TEAM MEMBER

W.T.A.G. (WORKED TOWARD ANNUAL GOAL) SCORE 1- 10 BELOW ANNUAL GOAL:

LIST & SCORE OPPORTUNITIES

WEEK 1: WTAG SCORE

- ☐
- ☐
- ☐
- ☐

WEEK 2: WTAG SCORE

- ☐
- ☐
- ☐
- ☐

WEEK 3: WTAG SCORE

- ☐
- ☐
- ☐
- ☐

WEEK 4: WTAG SCORE

- ☐
- ☐
- ☐
- ☐

WEEK 5: WTAG SCORE

- ☐
- ☐
- ☐
- ☐

LIST & SCORE POSITIVES

WEEK 1: WTAG SCORE

- ☐
- ☐
- ☐
- ☐

WEEK 2: WTAG SCORE

- ☐
- ☐
- ☐
- ☐

WEEK 3: WTAG SCORE

- ☐
- ☐
- ☐
- ☐

WEEK 4: WTAG SCORE

- ☐
- ☐
- ☐
- ☐

WEEK 5: WTAG SCORE

- ☐
- ☐
- ☐
- ☐

WEEKLY TEAM MEMBER

W.T.A.G. (WORKED TOWARD ANNUAL GOAL) SCORE 1- 10 BELOW ANNUAL GOAL:

LIST & SCORE OPPORTUNITIES

WEEK 1: WTAG SCORE

- [ ]
- [ ]
- [ ]
- [ ]

WEEK 2: WTAG SCORE

- [ ]
- [ ]
- [ ]
- [ ]

WEEK 3: WTAG SCORE

- [ ]
- [ ]
- [ ]
- [ ]

WEEK 4: WTAG SCORE

- [ ]
- [ ]
- [ ]
- [ ]

WEEK 5: WTAG SCORE

- [ ]
- [ ]
- [ ]
- [ ]

LIST & SCORE POSITIVES

WEEK 1: WTAG SCORE

- [ ]
- [ ]
- [ ]
- [ ]

WEEK 2: WTAG SCORE

- [ ]
- [ ]
- [ ]
- [ ]

WEEK 3: WTAG SCORE

- [ ]
- [ ]
- [ ]
- [ ]

WEEK 4: WTAG SCORE

- [ ]
- [ ]
- [ ]
- [ ]

WEEK 5: WTAG SCORE

- [ ]
- [ ]
- [ ]
- [ ]

WEEKLY TEAM MEMBER

____

W.T.A.G. (WORKED TOWARD ANNUAL GOAL) SCORE 1- 10 BELOW ANNUAL GOAL: ______________________________

____

LIST & SCORE OPPORTUNITIES

WEEK 1: WTAG SCORE ______________

- ☐ ______________________________
- ☐ ______________________________
- ☐ ______________________________
- ☐ ______________________________

WEEK 2: WTAG SCORE ______________

- ☐ ______________________________
- ☐ ______________________________
- ☐ ______________________________
- ☐ ______________________________

WEEK 3: WTAG SCORE ______________

- ☐ ______________________________
- ☐ ______________________________
- ☐ ______________________________
- ☐ ______________________________

WEEK 4: WTAG SCORE ______________

- ☐ ______________________________
- ☐ ______________________________
- ☐ ______________________________
- ☐ ______________________________

WEEK 5: WTAG SCORE ______________

- ☐ ______________________________
- ☐ ______________________________
- ☐ ______________________________
- ☐ ______________________________

LIST & SCORE POSITIVES

WEEK 1: WTAG SCORE ______________

- ☐ ______________________________
- ☐ ______________________________
- ☐ ______________________________
- ☐ ______________________________

WEEK 2: WTAG SCORE ______________

- ☐ ______________________________
- ☐ ______________________________
- ☐ ______________________________
- ☐ ______________________________

WEEK 3: WTAG SCORE ______________

- ☐ ______________________________
- ☐ ______________________________
- ☐ ______________________________
- ☐ ______________________________

WEEK 4: WTAG SCORE ______________

- ☐ ______________________________
- ☐ ______________________________
- ☐ ______________________________
- ☐ ______________________________

WEEK 5: WTAG SCORE ______________

- ☐ ______________________________
- ☐ ______________________________
- ☐ ______________________________
- ☐ ______________________________

Weekly Team Member

W.T.A.G. (WORKED TOWARD ANNUAL GOAL) SCORE 1- 10 BELOW ANNUAL GOAL:

List & score opportunities

WEEK 1: WTAG SCORE

- ☐
- ☐
- ☐
- ☐

WEEK 2: WTAG SCORE

- ☐
- ☐
- ☐
- ☐

WEEK 3: WTAG SCORE

- ☐
- ☐
- ☐
- ☐

WEEK 4: WTAG SCORE

- ☐
- ☐
- ☐
- ☐

WEEK 5: WTAG SCORE

- ☐
- ☐
- ☐
- ☐

List & score Positives

WEEK 1: WTAG SCORE

- ☐
- ☐
- ☐
- ☐

WEEK 2: WTAG SCORE

- ☐
- ☐
- ☐
- ☐

WEEK 3: WTAG SCORE

- ☐
- ☐
- ☐
- ☐

WEEK 4: WTAG SCORE

- ☐
- ☐
- ☐
- ☐

WEEK 5: WTAG SCORE

- ☐
- ☐
- ☐
- ☐

WEEKLY TEAM MEMBER

W.T.A.G. (WORKED TOWARD ANNUAL GOAL) SCORE 1- 10 BELOW ANNUAL GOAL: ____________

LIST & SCORE OPPORTUNITIES

WEEK 1: WTAG SCORE ____________

- [ ] ____________
- [ ] ____________
- [ ] ____________
- [ ] ____________

WEEK 2: WTAG SCORE ____________

- [ ] ____________
- [ ] ____________
- [ ] ____________
- [ ] ____________

WEEK 3: WTAG SCORE ____________

- [ ] ____________
- [ ] ____________
- [ ] ____________
- [ ] ____________

WEEK 4: WTAG SCORE ____________

- [ ] ____________
- [ ] ____________
- [ ] ____________
- [ ] ____________

WEEK 5: WTAG SCORE ____________

- [ ] ____________
- [ ] ____________
- [ ] ____________
- [ ] ____________

LIST & SCORE POSITIVES

WEEK 1: WTAG SCORE ____________

- [ ] ____________
- [ ] ____________
- [ ] ____________
- [ ] ____________

WEEK 2: WTAG SCORE ____________

- [ ] ____________
- [ ] ____________
- [ ] ____________
- [ ] ____________

WEEK 3: WTAG SCORE ____________

- [ ] ____________
- [ ] ____________
- [ ] ____________
- [ ] ____________

WEEK 4: WTAG SCORE ____________

- [ ] ____________
- [ ] ____________
- [ ] ____________
- [ ] ____________

WEEK 5: WTAG SCORE ____________

- [ ] ____________
- [ ] ____________
- [ ] ____________
- [ ] ____________

WEEKLY TEAM MEMBER

W.T.A.G. (WORKED TOWARD ANNUAL GOAL) SCORE 1- 10 BELOW ANNUAL GOAL:

LIST & SCORE OPPORTUNITIES

WEEK 1: WTAG SCORE

- [ ]
- [ ]
- [ ]
- [ ]

WEEK 2: WTAG SCORE

- [ ]
- [ ]
- [ ]
- [ ]

WEEK 3: WTAG SCORE

- [ ]
- [ ]
- [ ]
- [ ]

WEEK 4: WTAG SCORE

- [ ]
- [ ]
- [ ]
- [ ]

WEEK 5: WTAG SCORE

- [ ]
- [ ]
- [ ]
- [ ]

LIST & SCORE POSITIVES

WEEK 1: WTAG SCORE

- [ ]
- [ ]
- [ ]
- [ ]

WEEK 2: WTAG SCORE

- [ ]
- [ ]
- [ ]
- [ ]

WEEK 3: WTAG SCORE

- [ ]
- [ ]
- [ ]
- [ ]

WEEK 4: WTAG SCORE

- [ ]
- [ ]
- [ ]
- [ ]

WEEK 5: WTAG SCORE

- [ ]
- [ ]
- [ ]
- [ ]

WEEKLY TEAM MEMBER

W.T.A.G. (WORKED TOWARD ANNUAL GOAL) SCORE 1- 10 BELOW ANNUAL GOAL: ____________

____

LIST & SCORE OPPORTUNITIES

WEEK 1: WTAG SCORE ____________

- ☐ ____________
- ☐ ____________
- ☐ ____________
- ☐ ____________

WEEK 2: WTAG SCORE ____________

- ☐ ____________
- ☐ ____________
- ☐ ____________
- ☐ ____________

WEEK 3: WTAG SCORE ____________

- ☐ ____________
- ☐ ____________
- ☐ ____________
- ☐ ____________

WEEK 4: WTAG SCORE ____________

- ☐ ____________
- ☐ ____________
- ☐ ____________
- ☐ ____________

WEEK 5: WTAG SCORE ____________

- ☐ ____________
- ☐ ____________
- ☐ ____________
- ☐ ____________

LIST & SCORE POSITIVES

WEEK 1: WTAG SCORE ____________

- ☐ ____________
- ☐ ____________
- ☐ ____________
- ☐ ____________

WEEK 2: WTAG SCORE ____________

- ☐ ____________
- ☐ ____________
- ☐ ____________
- ☐ ____________

WEEK 3: WTAG SCORE ____________

- ☐ ____________
- ☐ ____________
- ☐ ____________
- ☐ ____________

WEEK 4: WTAG SCORE ____________

- ☐ ____________
- ☐ ____________
- ☐ ____________
- ☐ ____________

WEEK 5: WTAG SCORE ____________

- ☐ ____________
- ☐ ____________
- ☐ ____________
- ☐ ____________

WEEKLY TEAM MEMBER

____

W.T.A.G. (WORKED TOWARD ANNUAL GOAL) SCORE 1- 10 BELOW ANNUAL GOAL: ______________

____

LIST & SCORE OPPORTUNITIES

WEEK 1: WTAG SCORE ______________

- [ ] ______________
- [ ] ______________
- [ ] ______________
- [ ] ______________

WEEK 2: WTAG SCORE ______________

- [ ] ______________
- [ ] ______________
- [ ] ______________
- [ ] ______________

WEEK 3: WTAG SCORE ______________

- [ ] ______________
- [ ] ______________
- [ ] ______________
- [ ] ______________

WEEK 4: WTAG SCORE ______________

- [ ] ______________
- [ ] ______________
- [ ] ______________
- [ ] ______________

WEEK 5: WTAG SCORE ______________

- [ ] ______________
- [ ] ______________
- [ ] ______________
- [ ] ______________

LIST & SCORE POSITIVES

WEEK 1: WTAG SCORE ______________

- [ ] ______________
- [ ] ______________
- [ ] ______________
- [ ] ______________

WEEK 2: WTAG SCORE ______________

- [ ] ______________
- [ ] ______________
- [ ] ______________
- [ ] ______________

WEEK 3: WTAG SCORE ______________

- [ ] ______________
- [ ] ______________
- [ ] ______________
- [ ] ______________

WEEK 4: WTAG SCORE ______________

- [ ] ______________
- [ ] ______________
- [ ] ______________
- [ ] ______________

WEEK 5: WTAG SCORE ______________

- [ ] ______________
- [ ] ______________
- [ ] ______________
- [ ] ______________

WEEKLY TEAM MEMBER

____

W.T.A.G. (WORKED TOWARD ANNUAL GOAL) SCORE 1- 10 BELOW ANNUAL GOAL: ____________

____

LIST & SCORE OPPORTUNITIES

WEEK 1: WTAG SCORE ____________

- ☐ ____________
- ☐ ____________
- ☐ ____________
- ☐ ____________

WEEK 2: WTAG SCORE ____________

- ☐ ____________
- ☐ ____________
- ☐ ____________
- ☐ ____________

WEEK 3: WTAG SCORE ____________

- ☐ ____________
- ☐ ____________
- ☐ ____________
- ☐ ____________

WEEK 4: WTAG SCORE ____________

- ☐ ____________
- ☐ ____________
- ☐ ____________
- ☐ ____________

WEEK 5: WTAG SCORE ____________

- ☐ ____________
- ☐ ____________
- ☐ ____________
- ☐ ____________

LIST & SCORE POSITIVES

WEEK 1: WTAG SCORE ____________

- ☐ ____________
- ☐ ____________
- ☐ ____________
- ☐ ____________

WEEK 2: WTAG SCORE ____________

- ☐ ____________
- ☐ ____________
- ☐ ____________
- ☐ ____________

WEEK 3: WTAG SCORE ____________

- ☐ ____________
- ☐ ____________
- ☐ ____________
- ☐ ____________

WEEK 4: WTAG SCORE ____________

- ☐ ____________
- ☐ ____________
- ☐ ____________
- ☐ ____________

WEEK 5: WTAG SCORE ____________

- ☐ ____________
- ☐ ____________
- ☐ ____________
- ☐ ____________

Weekly Team Member

W.T.A.G. (WORKED TOWARD ANNUAL GOAL) SCORE 1- 10 BELOW ANNUAL GOAL:

List & score opportunities

WEEK 1: WTAG SCORE

- [ ]
- [ ]
- [ ]
- [ ]

WEEK 2: WTAG SCORE

- [ ]
- [ ]
- [ ]
- [ ]

WEEK 3: WTAG SCORE

- [ ]
- [ ]
- [ ]
- [ ]

WEEK 4: WTAG SCORE

- [ ]
- [ ]
- [ ]
- [ ]

WEEK 5: WTAG SCORE

- [ ]
- [ ]
- [ ]
- [ ]

List & score Positives

WEEK 1: WTAG SCORE

- [ ]
- [ ]
- [ ]
- [ ]

WEEK 2: WTAG SCORE

- [ ]
- [ ]
- [ ]
- [ ]

WEEK 3: WTAG SCORE

- [ ]
- [ ]
- [ ]
- [ ]

WEEK 4: WTAG SCORE

- [ ]
- [ ]
- [ ]
- [ ]

WEEK 5: WTAG SCORE

- [ ]
- [ ]
- [ ]
- [ ]

WEEKLY TEAM MEMBER

W.T.A.G. (WORKED TOWARD ANNUAL GOAL) SCORE 1- 10 BELOW ANNUAL GOAL:

LIST & SCORE OPPORTUNITIES

WEEK 1: WTAG SCORE

- ☐
- ☐
- ☐
- ☐

WEEK 2: WTAG SCORE

- ☐
- ☐
- ☐
- ☐

WEEK 3: WTAG SCORE

- ☐
- ☐
- ☐
- ☐

WEEK 4: WTAG SCORE

- ☐
- ☐
- ☐
- ☐

WEEK 5: WTAG SCORE

- ☐
- ☐
- ☐
- ☐

LIST & SCORE POSITIVES

WEEK 1: WTAG SCORE

- ☐
- ☐
- ☐
- ☐

WEEK 2: WTAG SCORE

- ☐
- ☐
- ☐
- ☐

WEEK 3: WTAG SCORE

- ☐
- ☐
- ☐
- ☐

WEEK 4: WTAG SCORE

- ☐
- ☐
- ☐
- ☐

WEEK 5: WTAG SCORE

- ☐
- ☐
- ☐
- ☐

WEEKLY TEAM MEMBER

____

W.T.A.G. (WORKED TOWARD ANNUAL GOAL) SCORE 1- 10 BELOW ANNUAL GOAL: ______________________________

____

LIST & SCORE OPPORTUNITIES

WEEK 1: WTAG SCORE ______

- [ ] ______
- [ ] ______
- [ ] ______
- [ ] ______

WEEK 2: WTAG SCORE ______

- [ ] ______
- [ ] ______
- [ ] ______
- [ ] ______

WEEK 3: WTAG SCORE ______

- [ ] ______
- [ ] ______
- [ ] ______
- [ ] ______

WEEK 4: WTAG SCORE ______

- [ ] ______
- [ ] ______
- [ ] ______
- [ ] ______

WEEK 5: WTAG SCORE ______

- [ ] ______
- [ ] ______
- [ ] ______
- [ ] ______

LIST & SCORE POSITIVES

WEEK 1: WTAG SCORE ______

- [ ] ______
- [ ] ______
- [ ] ______
- [ ] ______

WEEK 2: WTAG SCORE ______

- [ ] ______
- [ ] ______
- [ ] ______
- [ ] ______

WEEK 3: WTAG SCORE ______

- [ ] ______
- [ ] ______
- [ ] ______
- [ ] ______

WEEK 4: WTAG SCORE ______

- [ ] ______
- [ ] ______
- [ ] ______
- [ ] ______

WEEK 5: WTAG SCORE ______

- [ ] ______
- [ ] ______
- [ ] ______
- [ ] ______

WEEKLY TEAM MEMBER

____

W.T.A.G. (WORKED TOWARD ANNUAL GOAL) SCORE 1- 10 BELOW ANNUAL GOAL: ____________

____

LIST & SCORE OPPORTUNITIES

WEEK 1: WTAG SCORE ________

- ▢ ____________
- ▢ ____________
- ▢ ____________
- ▢ ____________

WEEK 2: WTAG SCORE ________

- ▢ ____________
- ▢ ____________
- ▢ ____________
- ▢ ____________

WEEK 3: WTAG SCORE ________

- ▢ ____________
- ▢ ____________
- ▢ ____________
- ▢ ____________

WEEK 4: WTAG SCORE ________

- ▢ ____________
- ▢ ____________
- ▢ ____________
- ▢ ____________

WEEK 5: WTAG SCORE ________

- ▢ ____________
- ▢ ____________
- ▢ ____________
- ▢ ____________

LIST & SCORE POSITIVES

WEEK 1: WTAG SCORE ________

- ▢ ____________
- ▢ ____________
- ▢ ____________
- ▢ ____________

WEEK 2: WTAG SCORE ________

- ▢ ____________
- ▢ ____________
- ▢ ____________
- ▢ ____________

WEEK 3: WTAG SCORE ________

- ▢ ____________
- ▢ ____________
- ▢ ____________
- ▢ ____________

WEEK 4: WTAG SCORE ________

- ▢ ____________
- ▢ ____________
- ▢ ____________
- ▢ ____________

WEEK 5: WTAG SCORE ________

- ▢ ____________
- ▢ ____________
- ▢ ____________
- ▢ ____________

TEAM MEETING

WEEK: ____________

WINS/SUCCESSES

OPPORTUNITIES FOR IMPROVEMENT

PROJECTIONS & MONTHLY GOAL TRACKING

NEW PATIENTS: ____________

CAPTURE RATE: ____________

AVERAGE SALE: ____________

STAFF PRODUCTIVITY: ____________

WEEKLY CHECKLIST TO ACHIEVE MONTHLY GOAL

- ☐ ____________
- ☐ ____________
- ☐ ____________
- ☐ ____________

NOTES

DAILY PERSONAL PLANNER

DATE: ____________________ S M T W T F S

Failure is simply the opportunity to begin again, this time more intelligently"
- Henry Ford.

TODAY'S SCHEDULE

6:00 ____________________
7:00 ____________________
8:00 ____________________
9:00 ____________________
10:00 ____________________
11:00 ____________________
12:00 ____________________
13:00 ____________________
14:00 ____________________
15:00 ____________________
16:00 ____________________
17:00 ____________________
18:00 ____________________
19:00 ____________________
20:00 ____________________
21:00 ____________________
22:00 ____________________

ACTION PLAN (TOP 3 PRIORITIES)

- ☐ ____________________
- ☐ ____________________
- ☐ ____________________

TASKS

- ☐ ____________________
- ☐ ____________________
- ☐ ____________________

WORK OUT COMPLETE

- ☐

WATER INTAKE

BREAKFAST PLAN ____________________

LUNCH PLAN ____________________

DINNER PLAN ____________________

HOURS SLEPT ____________________

END OF DAY REFLECTION: CELEBRATE TEAM MEMBERS & DAILY SUCCESS

____

____

END OF DAY REFLECTION: WHAT NEEDS IMPROVEMENT?

____

____

Daily Personal Planner

DATE: ____________________ S M T W T F S

"Your most unhappy patient is your greatest source of learning"
- Bill Gates

Today's Schedule

6:00

7:00

8:00

9:00

10:00

11:00

12:00

13:00

14:00

15:00

16:00

17:00

18:00

19:00

20:00

21:00

22:00

Action Plan (Top 3 priorities)

- ▢
- ▢
- ▢

TASKS

- ▢
- ▢
- ▢

WORK OUT COMPLETE

▢

WATER INTAKE

Breakfast Plan

Lunch Plan

Dinner Plan

Hours Slept

End of Day Reflection: Celebrate Team members & Daily success

End of Day Reflection: what needs improvement?

DAILY PERSONAL PLANNER

DATE: ____________________ S M T W T F S

"The way to get started is to quit talking and begin doing."
- Walt Disney

TODAY'S SCHEDULE

6:00 ____________________
7:00 ____________________
8:00 ____________________
9:00 ____________________
10:00 ____________________
11:00 ____________________
12:00 ____________________
13:00 ____________________
14:00 ____________________
15:00 ____________________
16:00 ____________________
17:00 ____________________
18:00 ____________________
19:00 ____________________
20:00 ____________________
21:00 ____________________
22:00 ____________________

ACTION PLAN (TOP 3 PRIORITIES)

- ☐ ____________________
- ☐ ____________________
- ☐ ____________________

TASKS

- ☐ ____________________
- ☐ ____________________
- ☐ ____________________

WORK OUT COMPLETE

☐

WATER INTAKE

BREAKFAST PLAN ____________________

LUNCH PLAN ____________________

DINNER PLAN ____________________

HOURS SLEPT ____________________

END OF DAY REFLECTION: CELEBRATE TEAM MEMBERS & DAILY SUCCESS

____

____

END OF DAY REFLECTION: WHAT NEEDS IMPROVEMENT?

____

____

DAILY PERSONAL PLANNER

DATE: ____________________ S M T W T F S

"Whether you think you can or you can't, you're right"
- Henry Ford

TODAY'S SCHEDULE

6:00
7:00
8:00
9:00
10:00
11:00
12:00
13:00
14:00
15:00
16:00
17:00
18:00
19:00
20:00
21:00
22:00

ACTION PLAN (TOP 3 PRIORITIES)

- ▢
- ▢
- ▢

TASKS

- ▢
- ▢
- ▢

WORK OUT COMPLETE

▢

WATER INTAKE

BREAKFAST PLAN

LUNCH PLAN

DINNER PLAN

HOURS SLEPT

END OF DAY REFLECTION: CELEBRATE TEAM MEMBERS & DAILY SUCCESS

END OF DAY REFLECTION: WHAT NEEDS IMPROVEMENT?

Daily Personal Planner

Date: ____________________ S M T W T F S

Innovation distinguishes between a leader and a follower"
- Steve Jobs

Today's Schedule

6:00

7:00

8:00

9:00

10:00

11:00

12:00

13:00

14:00

15:00

16:00

17:00

18:00

19:00

20:00

21:00

22:00

Action Plan (Top 3 priorities)

- ☐
- ☐
- ☐

Tasks

- ☐
- ☐
- ☐

Work Out Complete

☐

Water Intake

Breakfast Plan

Lunch Plan

Dinner Plan

Hours Slept

End of Day Reflection: Celebrate Team members & Daily success

End of Day Reflection: what needs improvement?

DAILY PERSONAL PLANNER

DATE: ____________ S M T W T F S

"Successful entrepreneurs are lifelong learners who are constantly looking for ways to improve and grow".
- Unknown

TODAY'S SCHEDULE

6:00 ____
7:00 ____
8:00 ____
9:00 ____
10:00 ____
11:00 ____
12:00 ____
13:00 ____
14:00 ____
15:00 ____
16:00 ____
17:00 ____
18:00 ____
19:00 ____
20:00 ____
21:00 ____
22:00 ____

ACTION PLAN (TOP 3 PRIORITIES)

- ☐ ____
- ☐ ____
- ☐ ____

TASKS

- ☐ ____
- ☐ ____
- ☐ ____

WORK OUT COMPLETE

- ☐

WATER INTAKE

BREAKFAST PLAN ____

LUNCH PLAN ____

DINNER PLAN ____

HOURS SLEPT ____

END OF DAY REFLECTION: CELEBRATE TEAM MEMBERS & DAILY SUCCESS

____

____

END OF DAY REFLECTION: WHAT NEEDS IMPROVEMENT?

____

____

DAILY PERSONAL PLANNER

DATE: ____________________ S M T W T F S

"Successful entrepreneurs don't wait for opportunities; they create them"
- Unknown

TODAY'S SCHEDULE

6:00
7:00
8:00
9:00
10:00
11:00
12:00
13:00
14:00
15:00
16:00
17:00
18:00
19:00
20:00
21:00
22:00

ACTION PLAN (TOP 3 PRIORITIES)

- ☐
- ☐
- ☐

TASKS

- ☐
- ☐
- ☐

WORK OUT COMPLETE

☐

WATER INTAKE

BREAKFAST PLAN

LUNCH PLAN

DINNER PLAN

HOURS SLEPT

END OF DAY REFLECTION: CELEBRATE TEAM MEMBERS & DAILY SUCCESS

END OF DAY REFLECTION: WHAT NEEDS IMPROVEMENT?

Team Meeting

Week: ____________

WINS/SUCCESSES

OPPORTUNITIES FOR IMPROVEMENT

Projections & Monthly Goal Tracking

New Patients: ____________

Capture Rate: ____________

Average Sale: ____________

Staff Productivity: ____________

Weekly Checklist to Achieve Monthly Goal

- [ ] ____________
- [ ] ____________
- [ ] ____________
- [ ] ____________

Notes

DAILY PERSONAL PLANNER

DATE: ____________________ S M T W T F S

"A successful business is built on passion and hard work"
- Unknown

TODAY'S SCHEDULE

6:00 ____
7:00 ____
8:00 ____
9:00 ____
10:00 ____
11:00 ____
12:00 ____
13:00 ____
14:00 ____
15:00 ____
16:00 ____
17:00 ____
18:00 ____
19:00 ____
20:00 ____
21:00 ____
22:00 ____

ACTION PLAN (TOP 3 PRIORITIES)

- ☐ ____
- ☐ ____
- ☐ ____

TASKS

- ☐ ____
- ☐ ____
- ☐ ____

WORK OUT COMPLETE

☐

WATER INTAKE

BREAKFAST PLAN ____

LUNCH PLAN ____

DINNER PLAN ____

HOURS SLEPT ____

END OF DAY REFLECTION: CELEBRATE TEAM MEMBERS & DAILY SUCCESS

____

____

END OF DAY REFLECTION: WHAT NEEDS IMPROVEMENT?

____

____

Daily Personal Planner

DATE: ________________ S M T W T F S

"It does not matter how slowly you go so long as you do not stop"
- Confucious

Today's Schedule

6:00

7:00

8:00

9:00

10:00

11:00

12:00

13:00

14:00

15:00

16:00

17:00

18:00

19:00

20:00

21:00

22:00

Action Plan (Top 3 priorities)

- ▢
- ▢
- ▢

TASKS

- ▢
- ▢
- ▢

WORK OUT COMPLETE

- ▢

WATER INTAKE

Breakfast Plan

Lunch Plan

Dinner Plan

Hours Slept

End of Day Reflection: Celebrate Team members & Daily success

End of Day Reflection: what needs improvement?

Daily Personal Planner

DATE: ______________________ S M T W T F S

"There are no secrets to success. It is the result of preparation, hard work, and learning from failure"
- Colin Powell

Today's Schedule

6:00
7:00
8:00
9:00
10:00
11:00
12:00
13:00
14:00
15:00
16:00
17:00
18:00
19:00
20:00
21:00
22:00

Action Plan (Top 3 priorities)

- ☐
- ☐
- ☐

TASKS

- ☐
- ☐
- ☐

WORK OUT COMPLETE

- ☐

WATER INTAKE

Breakfast Plan ______________

Lunch Plan ______________

Dinner Plan ______________

Hours Slept ______________

End of Day Reflection: Celebrate Team members & Daily success

End of Day Reflection: what needs improvement?

DAILY PERSONAL PLANNER

DATE: ______________ S M T W T F S

"The best way to predict the future is to create it."
- Abraham Lincoln

TODAY'S SCHEDULE

6:00
7:00
8:00
9:00
10:00
11:00
12:00
13:00
14:00
15:00
16:00
17:00
18:00
19:00
20:00
21:00
22:00

ACTION PLAN (TOP 3 PRIORITIES)

- ☐
- ☐
- ☐

TASKS

- ☐
- ☐
- ☐

WORK OUT COMPLETE

- ☐

WATER INTAKE

BREAKFAST PLAN

LUNCH PLAN

DINNER PLAN

HOURS SLEPT

END OF DAY REFLECTION: CELEBRATE TEAM MEMBERS & DAILY SUCCESS

END OF DAY REFLECTION: WHAT NEEDS IMPROVEMENT?

DAILY PERSONAL PLANNER

DATE: ______________________ S M T W T F S

"Your work is going to fill a large part of your life, and the only way to be truly satisfied is to do what you believe is great work. And the only way to do great work is to love what you do." - Steve Jobs

TODAY'S SCHEDULE

6:00 ____________________
7:00 ____________________
8:00 ____________________
9:00 ____________________
10:00 ____________________
11:00 ____________________
12:00 ____________________
13:00 ____________________
14:00 ____________________
15:00 ____________________
16:00 ____________________
17:00 ____________________
18:00 ____________________
19:00 ____________________
20:00 ____________________
21:00 ____________________
22:00 ____________________

ACTION PLAN (TOP 3 PRIORITIES)

- ☐ ____________________
- ☐ ____________________
- ☐ ____________________

TASKS

- ☐ ____________________
- ☐ ____________________
- ☐ ____________________

WORK OUT COMPLETE

☐

WATER INTAKE

BREAKFAST PLAN ____________________

LUNCH PLAN ____________________

DINNER PLAN ____________________

HOURS SLEPT ____________________

END OF DAY REFLECTION: CELEBRATE TEAM MEMBERS & DAILY SUCCESS

____

____

END OF DAY REFLECTION: WHAT NEEDS IMPROVEMENT?

____

____

DAILY PERSONAL PLANNER

DATE: ____________________ S M T W T F S

"Don't wait for opportunities, create them."
- Charles R. Schwab

TODAY'S SCHEDULE

6:00
7:00
8:00
9:00
10:00
11:00
12:00
13:00
14:00
15:00
16:00
17:00
18:00
19:00
20:00
21:00
22:00

ACTION PLAN (TOP 3 PRIORITIES)

- ☐
- ☐
- ☐

TASKS

- ☐
- ☐
- ☐

WORK OUT COMPLETE

- ☐

WATER INTAKE

BREAKFAST PLAN

LUNCH PLAN

DINNER PLAN

HOURS SLEPT

END OF DAY REFLECTION: CELEBRATE TEAM MEMBERS & DAILY SUCCESS

END OF DAY REFLECTION: WHAT NEEDS IMPROVEMENT?

Daily Personal Planner

DATE: ____________ S M T W T F S

"The biggest risk is not taking any risk. In a world that's changing quickly, the only strategy that is guaranteed to fail is not taking risks." - Mark Zuckerberg

Today's Schedule

6:00

7:00

8:00

9:00

10:00

11:00

12:00

13:00

14:00

15:00

16:00

17:00

18:00

19:00

20:00

21:00

22:00

Action Plan (Top 3 priorities)

- ☐
- ☐
- ☐

TASKS

- ☐
- ☐
- ☐

WORK OUT COMPLETE

☐

WATER INTAKE

Breakfast Plan ____________

Lunch Plan ____________

Dinner Plan ____________

Hours Slept ____________

End of Day Reflection: Celebrate Team members & Daily success

End of Day Reflection: what needs improvement?

TEAM MEETING

WEEK: ____________

WINS/SUCCESSES

OPPORTUNITIES FOR IMPROVEMENT

PROJECTIONS & MONTHLY GOAL TRACKING

NEW PATIENTS: ____________

CAPTURE RATE: ____________

AVERAGE SALE: ____________

STAFF PRODUCTIVITY: ____________

WEEKLY CHECKLIST TO ACHIEVE MONTHLY GOAL

- [ ] ____________
- [ ] ____________
- [ ] ____________
- [ ] ____________

NOTES

DAILY PERSONAL PLANNER

DATE: ______________________ S M T W T F S

"The biggest adventure you can ever take is to live the life of your dreams."
- Oprah Winfrey

TODAY'S SCHEDULE

6:00 ______
7:00 ______
8:00 ______
9:00 ______
10:00 ______
11:00 ______
12:00 ______
13:00 ______
14:00 ______
15:00 ______
16:00 ______
17:00 ______
18:00 ______
19:00 ______
20:00 ______
21:00 ______
22:00 ______

ACTION PLAN (TOP 3 PRIORITIES)

- ☐ ______
- ☐ ______
- ☐ ______

TASKS

- ☐ ______
- ☐ ______
- ☐ ______

WORK OUT COMPLETE

- ☐

WATER INTAKE

BREAKFAST PLAN ______

LUNCH PLAN ______

DINNER PLAN ______

HOURS SLEPT ______

END OF DAY REFLECTION: CELEBRATE TEAM MEMBERS & DAILY SUCCESS

______

______

END OF DAY REFLECTION: WHAT NEEDS IMPROVEMENT?

______

______

DAILY PERSONAL PLANNER

DATE: ______________________ S M T W T F S

"Success is not the key to happiness. Happiness is the key to success. If you love what you are doing, you will be successful." - Albert Schweitzer

TODAY'S SCHEDULE

6:00

7:00

8:00

9:00

10:00

11:00

12:00

13:00

14:00

15:00

16:00

17:00

18:00

19:00

20:00

21:00

22:00

ACTION PLAN (TOP 3 PRIORITIES)

- ☐
- ☐
- ☐

TASKS

- ☐
- ☐
- ☐

WORK OUT COMPLETE

- ☐

WATER INTAKE

BREAKFAST PLAN

LUNCH PLAN

DINNER PLAN

HOURS SLEPT

END OF DAY REFLECTION: CELEBRATE TEAM MEMBERS & DAILY SUCCESS

END OF DAY REFLECTION: WHAT NEEDS IMPROVEMENT?

Daily Personal Planner

DATE: ____________ S M T W T F S

"The only limit to our realization of tomorrow will be our doubts of today."
- Franklin D. Roosevelt

Today's Schedule

6:00
7:00
8:00
9:00
10:00
11:00
12:00
13:00
14:00
15:00
16:00
17:00
18:00
19:00
20:00
21:00
22:00

Action Plan (Top 3 priorities)

- ☐
- ☐
- ☐

TASKS

- ☐
- ☐
- ☐

WORK OUT COMPLETE

- ☐

WATER INTAKE

Breakfast Plan ____________

Lunch Plan ____________

Dinner Plan ____________

Hours Slept ____________

End of Day Reflection: Celebrate Team members & Daily success

End of Day Reflection: what needs improvement?

Daily Personal Planner

DATE: ____________________ S M T W T F S

"You miss 100% of the shots you don't take."
- Wayne Gretzky

Today's Schedule

6:00 ______
7:00 ______
8:00 ______
9:00 ______
10:00 ______
11:00 ______
12:00 ______
13:00 ______
14:00 ______
15:00 ______
16:00 ______
17:00 ______
18:00 ______
19:00 ______
20:00 ______
21:00 ______
22:00 ______

Action Plan (Top 3 priorities)

- [ ] ______
- [ ] ______
- [ ] ______

Tasks

- [ ] ______
- [ ] ______
- [ ] ______

Work out complete

- [ ]

Water intake

Breakfast Plan ______

Lunch Plan ______

Dinner Plan ______

Hours Slept ______

End of Day Reflection: Celebrate Team members & Daily success

______
______

End of Day Reflection: what needs improvement?

______
______

Daily Personal Planner

DATE: ____________________ S M T W T F S

"The best way to find yourself is to lose yourself in the service of others."
- Mahatma Gandhi

Today's Schedule

6:00

7:00

8:00

9:00

10:00

11:00

12:00

13:00

14:00

15:00

16:00

17:00

18:00

19:00

20:00

21:00

22:00

Action Plan (Top 3 priorities)

- [ ]
- [ ]
- [ ]

TASKS

- [ ]
- [ ]
- [ ]

WORK OUT COMPLETE

- [ ]

WATER INTAKE

Breakfast Plan

Lunch Plan

Dinner Plan

Hours Slept

End of Day Reflection: Celebrate Team members & Daily success

End of Day Reflection: what needs improvement?

DAILY PERSONAL PLANNER

DATE: ____________________ S M T W T F S

"The only way to do great work is to love what you do. If you haven't found it yet, keep looking. Don't settle. As with all matters of the heart, you'll know when you find it."
- Steve Jobs

TODAY'S SCHEDULE

6:00 ____________________
7:00 ____________________
8:00 ____________________
9:00 ____________________
10:00 ____________________
11:00 ____________________
12:00 ____________________
13:00 ____________________
14:00 ____________________
15:00 ____________________
16:00 ____________________
17:00 ____________________
18:00 ____________________
19:00 ____________________
20:00 ____________________
21:00 ____________________
22:00 ____________________

ACTION PLAN (TOP 3 PRIORITIES)

- ☐ ____________________
- ☐ ____________________
- ☐ ____________________

TASKS

- ☐ ____________________
- ☐ ____________________
- ☐ ____________________

WORK OUT COMPLETE

- ☐

WATER INTAKE

BREAKFAST PLAN ____________________

LUNCH PLAN ____________________

DINNER PLAN ____________________

HOURS SLEPT ____________________

END OF DAY REFLECTION: CELEBRATE TEAM MEMBERS & DAILY SUCCESS

____

____

END OF DAY REFLECTION: WHAT NEEDS IMPROVEMENT?

____

____

DAILY PERSONAL PLANNER

DATE: ______________ S M T W T F S

"The best time to plant a tree was 20 years ago. The second best time is now."
- Chinese Proverb

TODAY'S SCHEDULE

6:00
7:00
8:00
9:00
10:00
11:00
12:00
13:00
14:00
15:00
16:00
17:00
18:00
19:00
20:00
21:00
22:00

ACTION PLAN (TOP 3 PRIORITIES)

- ☐
- ☐
- ☐

TASKS

- ☐
- ☐
- ☐

WORK OUT COMPLETE

- ☐

WATER INTAKE

BREAKFAST PLAN

LUNCH PLAN

DINNER PLAN

HOURS SLEPT

END OF DAY REFLECTION: CELEBRATE TEAM MEMBERS & DAILY SUCCESS

END OF DAY REFLECTION: WHAT NEEDS IMPROVEMENT?

TEAM MEETING

WEEK: ____________

WINS/SUCCESSES

OPPORTUNITIES FOR IMPROVEMENT

PROJECTIONS & MONTHLY GOAL TRACKING

NEW PATIENTS: ____________

CAPTURE RATE: ____________

AVERAGE SALE: ____________

STAFF PRODUCTIVITY: ____________

WEEKLY CHECKLIST TO ACHIEVE MONTHLY GOAL

- ☐ ____________
- ☐ ____________
- ☐ ____________
- ☐ ____________

NOTES

Daily Personal Planner

DATE: ____________________ S M T W T F S

•"You can't build a reputation on what you are going to do."
- Henry Ford

Today's Schedule

6:00 ____________________
7:00 ____________________
8:00 ____________________
9:00 ____________________
10:00 ____________________
11:00 ____________________
12:00 ____________________
13:00 ____________________
14:00 ____________________
15:00 ____________________
16:00 ____________________
17:00 ____________________
18:00 ____________________
19:00 ____________________
20:00 ____________________
21:00 ____________________
22:00 ____________________

Action Plan (Top 3 priorities)

- ☐ ____________________
- ☐ ____________________
- ☐ ____________________

TASKS

- ☐ ____________________
- ☐ ____________________
- ☐ ____________________

WORK OUT COMPLETE

- ☐

WATER INTAKE

Breakfast Plan ____________________

Lunch Plan ____________________

Dinner Plan ____________________

Hours Slept ____________________

End of Day Reflection: Celebrate Team members & Daily success

____

____

End of Day Reflection: what needs improvement?

____

____

DAILY PERSONAL PLANNER

DATE: ______________________ S M T W T F S

"Your most unhappy patient is your greatest source of learning"
- Bill Gates

TODAY'S SCHEDULE

6:00 ______

7:00 ______

8:00 ______

9:00 ______

10:00 ______

11:00 ______

12:00 ______

13:00 ______

14:00 ______

15:00 ______

16:00 ______

17:00 ______

18:00 ______

19:00 ______

20:00 ______

21:00 ______

22:00 ______

ACTION PLAN (TOP 3 PRIORITIES)

- ☐ ______
- ☐ ______
- ☐ ______

TASKS

- ☐ ______
- ☐ ______
- ☐ ______

WORK OUT COMPLETE

- ☐

WATER INTAKE

BREAKFAST PLAN ______

LUNCH PLAN ______

DINNER PLAN ______

HOURS SLEPT ______

END OF DAY REFLECTION: CELEBRATE TEAM MEMBERS & DAILY SUCCESS

______

______

END OF DAY REFLECTION: WHAT NEEDS IMPROVEMENT?

______

______

DAILY PERSONAL PLANNER

DATE: ____________________ S M T W T F S

"Success is not final, failure is not fatal: It is the courage to continue that counts."
- Winston Churchill

TODAY'S SCHEDULE

6:00
7:00
8:00
9:00
10:00
11:00
12:00
13:00
14:00
15:00
16:00
17:00
18:00
19:00
20:00
21:00
22:00

ACTION PLAN (TOP 3 PRIORITIES)

- ☐
- ☐
- ☐

TASKS

- ☐
- ☐
- ☐

WORK OUT COMPLETE

☐

WATER INTAKE

BREAKFAST PLAN ____________________

LUNCH PLAN ____________________

DINNER PLAN ____________________

HOURS SLEPT ____________________

END OF DAY REFLECTION: CELEBRATE TEAM MEMBERS & DAILY SUCCESS

END OF DAY REFLECTION: WHAT NEEDS IMPROVEMENT?

DAILY PERSONAL PLANNER

DATE: ____________________ S M T W T F S

• *"The road to success and greatness is always paved with consistent hard work. Outwork your competitors and be relentless." – Unknown*

TODAY'S SCHEDULE

6:00

7:00

8:00

9:00

10:00

11:00

12:00

13:00

14:00

15:00

16:00

17:00

18:00

19:00

20:00

21:00

22:00

ACTION PLAN (TOP 3 PRIORITIES)

- ☐
- ☐
- ☐

TASKS

- ☐
- ☐
- ☐

WORK OUT COMPLETE

- ☐

WATER INTAKE

BREAKFAST PLAN ____________________

LUNCH PLAN ____________________

DINNER PLAN ____________________

HOURS SLEPT ____________________

END OF DAY REFLECTION: CELEBRATE TEAM MEMBERS & DAILY SUCCESS

END OF DAY REFLECTION: WHAT NEEDS IMPROVEMENT?

DAILY PERSONAL PLANNER

DATE: ____________ S M T W T F S

"Successful people do what unsuccessful people are not willing to do. Don't wish it were easier, wish you were better." –Jim Rohn

TODAY'S SCHEDULE

6:00
7:00
8:00
9:00
10:00
11:00
12:00
13:00
14:00
15:00
16:00
17:00
18:00
19:00
20:00
21:00
22:00

ACTION PLAN (TOP 3 PRIORITIES)

- ☐
- ☐
- ☐

TASKS

- ☐
- ☐
- ☐

WORK OUT COMPLETE

- ☐

WATER INTAKE

BREAKFAST PLAN

LUNCH PLAN

DINNER PLAN

HOURS SLEPT

END OF DAY REFLECTION: CELEBRATE TEAM MEMBERS & DAILY SUCCESS

END OF DAY REFLECTION: WHAT NEEDS IMPROVEMENT?

DAILY PERSONAL PLANNER

DATE: ____________________ S M T W T F S

"The best way to predict the future is to create it."
–Peter Drucker

TODAY'S SCHEDULE

6:00
7:00
8:00
9:00
10:00
11:00
12:00
13:00
14:00
15:00
16:00
17:00
18:00
19:00
20:00
21:00
22:00

ACTION PLAN (TOP 3 PRIORITIES)

- ☐
- ☐
- ☐

TASKS

- ☐
- ☐
- ☐

WORK OUT COMPLETE

- ☐

WATER INTAKE

BREAKFAST PLAN

LUNCH PLAN

DINNER PLAN

HOURS SLEPT

END OF DAY REFLECTION: CELEBRATE TEAM MEMBERS & DAILY SUCCESS

END OF DAY REFLECTION: WHAT NEEDS IMPROVEMENT?

DAILY PERSONAL PLANNER

DATE: ____________________ S M T W T F S

"You don't have to be great to start, but you have to start to be great."
–Zig Ziglar

TODAY'S SCHEDULE

6:00
7:00
8:00
9:00
10:00
11:00
12:00
13:00
14:00
15:00
16:00
17:00
18:00
19:00
20:00
21:00
22:00

ACTION PLAN (TOP 3 PRIORITIES)

- ☐
- ☐
- ☐

TASKS

- ☐
- ☐
- ☐

WORK OUT COMPLETE

☐

WATER INTAKE

BREAKFAST PLAN

LUNCH PLAN

DINNER PLAN

HOURS SLEPT

END OF DAY REFLECTION: CELEBRATE TEAM MEMBERS & DAILY SUCCESS

END OF DAY REFLECTION: WHAT NEEDS IMPROVEMENT?

Team Meeting

Week: ____________

WINS/SUCCESSES

OPPORTUNITIES FOR IMPROVEMENT

Projections & Monthly Goal Tracking

New Patients: ____________

Capture Rate: ____________

Average Sale: ____________

Staff Productivity: ____________

Weekly Checklist to Achieve Monthly Goal

- ☐ ____________
- ☐ ____________
- ☐ ____________
- ☐ ____________

Notes

Daily Personal Planner

Date: ____________________ S M T W T F S

"Success is walking from failure to failure with no loss of enthusiasm."
– Winston Churchill

Today's Schedule

6:00 ____________________

7:00 ____________________

8:00 ____________________

9:00 ____________________

10:00 ____________________

11:00 ____________________

12:00 ____________________

13:00 ____________________

14:00 ____________________

15:00 ____________________

16:00 ____________________

17:00 ____________________

18:00 ____________________

19:00 ____________________

20:00 ____________________

21:00 ____________________

22:00 ____________________

Action Plan (Top 3 priorities)

- ☐ ____________________
- ☐ ____________________
- ☐ ____________________

Tasks

- ☐ ____________________
- ☐ ____________________
- ☐ ____________________

Work out complete

- ☐

Water intake

Breakfast Plan ____________________

Lunch Plan ____________________

Dinner Plan ____________________

Hours Slept ____________________

End of Day Reflection: Celebrate Team members & Daily success

____

____

End of Day Reflection: what needs improvement?

____

____

Daily Personal Planner

DATE: ____________ S M T W T F S

"Don't be afraid to give up the good to go for the great."
– John D. Rockefeller

Today's Schedule

6:00
7:00
8:00
9:00
10:00
11:00
12:00
13:00
14:00
15:00
16:00
17:00
18:00
19:00
20:00
21:00
22:00

Action Plan (Top 3 priorities)

- ☐
- ☐
- ☐

TASKS

- ☐
- ☐
- ☐

WORK OUT COMPLETE

- ☐

WATER INTAKE

Breakfast Plan

Lunch Plan

Dinner Plan

Hours Slept

End of Day Reflection: Celebrate Team members & Daily success

End of Day Reflection: what needs improvement?

DAILY PERSONAL PLANNER

DATE: ____________________ S M T W T F S

"Success is not the key to happiness. Happiness is the key to success. If you love what you are doing, you will be successful." – Albert Schweitzer

TODAY'S SCHEDULE

6:00

7:00

8:00

9:00

10:00

11:00

12:00

13:00

14:00

15:00

16:00

17:00

18:00

19:00

20:00

21:00

22:00

ACTION PLAN (TOP 3 PRIORITIES)

- ☐
- ☐
- ☐

TASKS

- ☐
- ☐
- ☐

WORK OUT COMPLETE

☐

WATER INTAKE

BREAKFAST PLAN

LUNCH PLAN

DINNER PLAN

HOURS SLEPT

END OF DAY REFLECTION: CELEBRATE TEAM MEMBERS & DAILY SUCCESS

END OF DAY REFLECTION: WHAT NEEDS IMPROVEMENT?

Daily Personal Planner

DATE: ______________________ S M T W T F S

"The most difficult thing is the decision to act, the rest is merely tenacity."
– Amelia Earhart

Today's Schedule

6:00 ____
7:00 ____
8:00 ____
9:00 ____
10:00 ____
11:00 ____
12:00 ____
13:00 ____
14:00 ____
15:00 ____
16:00 ____
17:00 ____
18:00 ____
19:00 ____
20:00 ____
21:00 ____
22:00 ____

Action Plan (Top 3 priorities)

- ☐ ____
- ☐ ____
- ☐ ____

TASKS

- ☐ ____
- ☐ ____
- ☐ ____

WORK OUT COMPLETE

- ☐

WATER INTAKE

Breakfast Plan ____

Lunch Plan ____

Dinner Plan ____

Hours Slept ____

End of Day Reflection: Celebrate Team members & Daily success

____

End of Day Reflection: what needs improvement?

____

DAILY PERSONAL PLANNER

DATE: ______________________ S M T W T F S

"If you do what you've always done, you'll get what you've always gotten."
— Tony Robbins

TODAY'S SCHEDULE

6:00

7:00

8:00

9:00

10:00

11:00

12:00

13:00

14:00

15:00

16:00

17:00

18:00

19:00

20:00

21:00

22:00

ACTION PLAN (TOP 3 PRIORITIES)

- ☐
- ☐
- ☐

TASKS

- ☐
- ☐
- ☐

WORK OUT COMPLETE

☐

WATER INTAKE

BREAKFAST PLAN

LUNCH PLAN

DINNER PLAN

HOURS SLEPT

END OF DAY REFLECTION: CELEBRATE TEAM MEMBERS & DAILY SUCCESS

END OF DAY REFLECTION: WHAT NEEDS IMPROVEMENT?

Daily Personal Planner

Date: ____________________ S M T W T F S

"Be undeniably good. No marketing effort or social media buzzword can be a substitute for that." — Anthony Volodkin

Today's Schedule

6:00 ____________________

7:00 ____________________

8:00 ____________________

9:00 ____________________

10:00 ____________________

11:00 ____________________

12:00 ____________________

13:00 ____________________

14:00 ____________________

15:00 ____________________

16:00 ____________________

17:00 ____________________

18:00 ____________________

19:00 ____________________

20:00 ____________________

21:00 ____________________

22:00 ____________________

Action Plan (Top 3 priorities)

- ☐ ____________________
- ☐ ____________________
- ☐ ____________________

Tasks

- ☐ ____________________
- ☐ ____________________
- ☐ ____________________

Work out complete

☐

Water intake

Breakfast Plan ____________________

Lunch Plan ____________________

Dinner Plan ____________________

Hours Slept ____________________

End of Day Reflection: Celebrate Team members & Daily success

____

____

End of Day Reflection: what needs improvement?

____

____

Daily Personal Planner

DATE: ______________________ S M T W T F S

"You don't learn to walk by following rules. You learn by doing and falling over."
— Richard Branson

Today's Schedule

6:00 ____________________

7:00 ____________________

8:00 ____________________

9:00 ____________________

10:00 ____________________

11:00 ____________________

12:00 ____________________

13:00 ____________________

14:00 ____________________

15:00 ____________________

16:00 ____________________

17:00 ____________________

18:00 ____________________

19:00 ____________________

20:00 ____________________

21:00 ____________________

22:00 ____________________

Action Plan (Top 3 priorities)

- [ ] ____________________
- [ ] ____________________
- [ ] ____________________

Tasks

- [ ] ____________________
- [ ] ____________________
- [ ] ____________________

Work out complete

- [ ]

Water intake

Breakfast Plan ____________________

Lunch Plan ____________________

Dinner Plan ____________________

Hours Slept ____________________

End of Day Reflection: Celebrate Team members & Daily success

____

____

End of Day Reflection: what needs improvement?

____

____

MONTH:

SUN	MON	TUES	WED	THUR	FRI	SAT

MONTH GOALS

1. ______________________________

2. ______________________________

3. ______________________________

TO DO LIST

- ☐
- ☐
- ☐
- ☐
- ☐

MONTHLY PRACTICE MANAGEMENT

SHORT TERM

MONTH 1:

MONTH 2:

MONTH 3:

● SATISFIED ⊘ OKAY ⊗ DISSATISFIED

MONTHLY FINDINGS

1 2 3 4 5 6 7

8 9 10 11 12 13 14

15 16 17 18 19 20 21

22 23 24 25 26 27 28

29 30 31

Monthly Marketing One-Sheet

"By Failing to prepare, you are preparing to fail." –Benjamin Franklin

Concept & Initiation (What)
Name: ______
Goal: ______
Estimated Timeline: ______
Targets to Reach: ______

Define & Plan: (How)
Budget: ______

List requirements: ______

Materials Needed: ______

Actions Needed: ______

Launch & Execution: (Who, When & Where)
Project Manager: ______

Define Details needed for each action: ______

Create Plan To Execute: ______

Performance & Control
Plan Details in Timeline: ______

Communication Plan Used: ______

Measuring Success: ______

Project Close
Training Needed: ______

Implementation Process: ______

Assessment of Success

BENCHMARKS: PROFESSIONAL

	PRODUCTION YTD	COLLECTIONS YTD	NET
WEEK 1			
WEEK 2			
WEEK 3			
WEEK 4			
WEEK 5			

KEY
YTD: Year to Date
M: Month
Ins. Coll: Insurance Collections
PT. Coll: Patient Collections
NP EX.: New Patient Exams
EP EX.: Established Patient
Exams
Total EX.: Total Exams
Prod. EX.: Production Per Exam
Coll. EX.: Collection Per Exam
Prof. Fees: Professional Fees

M	INS. COLL.	PT. COLL.	NP EX.	EP EX.	TOTAL EX.	PRO/ EX.	COLL/ EX.	PROF. FEES	OTHER	OTHER	OTHER
1											
2											
3											
4											
5											
6											
7											
8											
9											
10											
11											
12											

Benchmarks: Retail

	Production YTD	Collections YTD	Net
Week 1			
Week 2			
Week 3			
Week 4			
Week 5			

KEY
YTD: Year to Date
M: Month
Ins. Coll: Insurance Collections
PT. Coll: Patient Collections
# of Frames: Number of Frames
Fr. Coll.: Frames Collected
Ave Fr Sale: Average Frame Sale
Lens Sold: Number of Lens Sold
Fr. Coll.: Frames Collected
Ave. Lens Sale: Average Lens Sale
Cap. Rate: Capture Rate
CL Fit Eval: Total Contact Lens Fits
CL Yr Supp: Contact Lens Year Supply
CL Capt. Rate: Contact Lens Capture Rate
CL Coll: Contact Lens Collections
CL$/Fit: Average Contact Lens Sale/Fitting

M	Ins. Coll.	Pt. Coll.	# of Frames	Fr Coll.	Ave Fr Sale	# Lens Sold	Fr Coll	Ave Lens Sale	Cap. Rate	CL Fit/ Eval	CL Yr Supp	CL Capt Rate	CL Coll	CL$ /Fit
1														
2														
3														
4														
5														
6														
7														
8														
9														
10														
11														
12														

Benchmarks: Special

	Production YTD	Collections YTD	Net
Week 1			
Week 2			
Week 3			
Week 4			
Week 5			

KEY
YTD: Year to Date
M: Month
Ins. Coll: Insurance Collections
PT. Coll: Patient Collections
VT Eval: Vision Therapy Evaluations
VT Conf: Vision Therapy Conferences
VT Sign-ups: Vision Therapy Sign-up
VT NS Rate: Vision Therapy No-show Rate
DE Eval: Vision Therapy Evaluations
DE Conf: Vision Therapy Conferences
DE Sign-ups: Vision Therapy Sign-up
CL Fit
CL Start: Contact Lens Starts
MD Eval: Macular Degeneration Evaluation
GL Eval: Glaucoma Evaluation
LV Eval: Low Vision Evaluation

M	Ins. Coll.	Pt. Coll.	VT Evals	VT Conf	VT Start	VT NS Rate	DE Eval	DE Conf	DE Start	CL Eval	MD Eval	GL Eval	LV Eval	Other
1														
2														
3														
4														
5														
6														
7														
8														
9														
10														
11														
12														

BENCHMARKS

INCOME

INCOME 1	
INCOME 2	
OTHER INCOME	
TOTAL	

EXPENSES

MONTH

BUDGET

TO BE PAID	DUE DATE	AMOUNT	PAID	NOTES

SUMMARY

TOTAL INCOME	TOTAL EXPENSES	DIFFERENCE

NOTES

Weekly Team Member

W.T.A.G. (WORKED TOWARD ANNUAL GOAL) SCORE 1- 10 BELOW ANNUAL GOAL:

List & score opportunities

WEEK 1: WTAG SCORE

- ☐
- ☐
- ☐
- ☐

WEEK 2: WTAG SCORE

- ☐
- ☐
- ☐
- ☐

WEEK 3: WTAG SCORE

- ☐
- ☐
- ☐
- ☐

WEEK 4: WTAG SCORE

- ☐
- ☐
- ☐
- ☐

WEEK 5: WTAG SCORE

- ☐
- ☐
- ☐
- ☐

List & score Positives

WEEK 1: WTAG SCORE

- ☐
- ☐
- ☐
- ☐

WEEK 2: WTAG SCORE

- ☐
- ☐
- ☐
- ☐

WEEK 3: WTAG SCORE

- ☐
- ☐
- ☐
- ☐

WEEK 4: WTAG SCORE

- ☐
- ☐
- ☐
- ☐

WEEK 5: WTAG SCORE

- ☐
- ☐
- ☐
- ☐

Weekly Team Member

W.T.A.G. (WORKED TOWARD ANNUAL GOAL) SCORE 1- 10 BELOW ANNUAL GOAL: ______

List & score opportunities

WEEK 1: WTAG SCORE ______

- [ ] ______
- [ ] ______
- [ ] ______
- [ ] ______

WEEK 2: WTAG SCORE ______

- [ ] ______
- [ ] ______
- [ ] ______
- [ ] ______

WEEK 3: WTAG SCORE ______

- [ ] ______
- [ ] ______
- [ ] ______
- [ ] ______

WEEK 4: WTAG SCORE ______

- [ ] ______
- [ ] ______
- [ ] ______
- [ ] ______

WEEK 5: WTAG SCORE ______

- [ ] ______
- [ ] ______
- [ ] ______
- [ ] ______

List & score Positives

WEEK 1: WTAG SCORE ______

- [ ] ______
- [ ] ______
- [ ] ______
- [ ] ______

WEEK 2: WTAG SCORE ______

- [ ] ______
- [ ] ______
- [ ] ______
- [ ] ______

WEEK 3: WTAG SCORE ______

- [ ] ______
- [ ] ______
- [ ] ______
- [ ] ______

WEEK 4: WTAG SCORE ______

- [ ] ______
- [ ] ______
- [ ] ______
- [ ] ______

WEEK 5: WTAG SCORE ______

- [ ] ______
- [ ] ______
- [ ] ______
- [ ] ______

WEEKLY TEAM MEMBER

W.T.A.G. (WORKED TOWARD ANNUAL GOAL) SCORE 1- 10 BELOW ANNUAL GOAL:

LIST & SCORE OPPORTUNITIES

WEEK 1: WTAG SCORE

- ☐
- ☐
- ☐
- ☐

WEEK 2: WTAG SCORE

- ☐
- ☐
- ☐
- ☐

WEEK 3: WTAG SCORE

- ☐
- ☐
- ☐
- ☐

WEEK 4: WTAG SCORE

- ☐
- ☐
- ☐
- ☐

WEEK 5: WTAG SCORE

- ☐
- ☐
- ☐
- ☐

LIST & SCORE POSITIVES

WEEK 1: WTAG SCORE

- ☐
- ☐
- ☐
- ☐

WEEK 2: WTAG SCORE

- ☐
- ☐
- ☐
- ☐

WEEK 3: WTAG SCORE

- ☐
- ☐
- ☐
- ☐

WEEK 4: WTAG SCORE

- ☐
- ☐
- ☐
- ☐

WEEK 5: WTAG SCORE

- ☐
- ☐
- ☐
- ☐

Weekly Team Member

W.T.A.G. (WORKED TOWARD ANNUAL GOAL) SCORE 1- 10 BELOW ANNUAL GOAL: ______

______

List & score opportunities

WEEK 1: WTAG SCORE ______

- ☐ ______
- ☐ ______
- ☐ ______
- ☐ ______

WEEK 2: WTAG SCORE ______

- ☐ ______
- ☐ ______
- ☐ ______
- ☐ ______

WEEK 3: WTAG SCORE ______

- ☐ ______
- ☐ ______
- ☐ ______
- ☐ ______

WEEK 4: WTAG SCORE ______

- ☐ ______
- ☐ ______
- ☐ ______
- ☐ ______

WEEK 5: WTAG SCORE ______

- ☐ ______
- ☐ ______
- ☐ ______
- ☐ ______

List & score Positives

WEEK 1: WTAG SCORE ______

- ☐ ______
- ☐ ______
- ☐ ______
- ☐ ______

WEEK 2: WTAG SCORE ______

- ☐ ______
- ☐ ______
- ☐ ______
- ☐ ______

WEEK 3: WTAG SCORE ______

- ☐ ______
- ☐ ______
- ☐ ______
- ☐ ______

WEEK 4: WTAG SCORE ______

- ☐ ______
- ☐ ______
- ☐ ______
- ☐ ______

WEEK 5: WTAG SCORE ______

- ☐ ______
- ☐ ______
- ☐ ______
- ☐ ______

Weekly Team Member

W.T.A.G. (WORKED TOWARD ANNUAL GOAL) SCORE 1- 10 BELOW ANNUAL GOAL: ____

List & score opportunities

WEEK 1: WTAG SCORE ____

- ☐ ____
- ☐ ____
- ☐ ____
- ☐ ____

WEEK 2: WTAG SCORE ____

- ☐ ____
- ☐ ____
- ☐ ____
- ☐ ____

WEEK 3: WTAG SCORE ____

- ☐ ____
- ☐ ____
- ☐ ____
- ☐ ____

WEEK 4: WTAG SCORE ____

- ☐ ____
- ☐ ____
- ☐ ____
- ☐ ____

WEEK 5: WTAG SCORE ____

- ☐ ____
- ☐ ____
- ☐ ____
- ☐ ____

List & score Positives

WEEK 1: WTAG SCORE ____

- ☐ ____
- ☐ ____
- ☐ ____
- ☐ ____

WEEK 2: WTAG SCORE ____

- ☐ ____
- ☐ ____
- ☐ ____
- ☐ ____

WEEK 3: WTAG SCORE ____

- ☐ ____
- ☐ ____
- ☐ ____
- ☐ ____

WEEK 4: WTAG SCORE ____

- ☐ ____
- ☐ ____
- ☐ ____
- ☐ ____

WEEK 5: WTAG SCORE ____

- ☐ ____
- ☐ ____
- ☐ ____
- ☐ ____

WEEKLY TEAM MEMBER

____

W.T.A.G. (WORKED TOWARD ANNUAL GOAL) SCORE 1- 10 BELOW ANNUAL GOAL: ____________

____

LIST & SCORE OPPORTUNITIES

WEEK 1: WTAG SCORE ____________

- ☐ ____________
- ☐ ____________
- ☐ ____________
- ☐ ____________

WEEK 2: WTAG SCORE ____________

- ☐ ____________
- ☐ ____________
- ☐ ____________
- ☐ ____________

WEEK 3: WTAG SCORE ____________

- ☐ ____________
- ☐ ____________
- ☐ ____________
- ☐ ____________

WEEK 4: WTAG SCORE ____________

- ☐ ____________
- ☐ ____________
- ☐ ____________
- ☐ ____________

WEEK 5: WTAG SCORE ____________

- ☐ ____________
- ☐ ____________
- ☐ ____________
- ☐ ____________

LIST & SCORE POSITIVES

WEEK 1: WTAG SCORE ____________

- ☐ ____________
- ☐ ____________
- ☐ ____________
- ☐ ____________

WEEK 2: WTAG SCORE ____________

- ☐ ____________
- ☐ ____________
- ☐ ____________
- ☐ ____________

WEEK 3: WTAG SCORE ____________

- ☐ ____________
- ☐ ____________
- ☐ ____________
- ☐ ____________

WEEK 4: WTAG SCORE ____________

- ☐ ____________
- ☐ ____________
- ☐ ____________
- ☐ ____________

WEEK 5: WTAG SCORE ____________

- ☐ ____________
- ☐ ____________
- ☐ ____________
- ☐ ____________

WEEKLY TEAM MEMBER

____

W.T.A.G. (WORKED TOWARD ANNUAL GOAL) SCORE 1- 10 BELOW ANNUAL GOAL: ____________

____

LIST & SCORE OPPORTUNITIES

WEEK 1: WTAG SCORE ____________

- [ ] ______________________
- [ ] ______________________
- [ ] ______________________
- [ ] ______________________

WEEK 2: WTAG SCORE ____________

- [ ] ______________________
- [ ] ______________________
- [ ] ______________________
- [ ] ______________________

WEEK 3: WTAG SCORE ____________

- [ ] ______________________
- [ ] ______________________
- [ ] ______________________
- [ ] ______________________

WEEK 4: WTAG SCORE ____________

- [ ] ______________________
- [ ] ______________________
- [ ] ______________________
- [ ] ______________________

WEEK 5: WTAG SCORE ____________

- [ ] ______________________
- [ ] ______________________
- [ ] ______________________
- [ ] ______________________

LIST & SCORE POSITIVES

WEEK 1: WTAG SCORE ____________

- [ ] ______________________
- [ ] ______________________
- [ ] ______________________
- [ ] ______________________

WEEK 2: WTAG SCORE ____________

- [ ] ______________________
- [ ] ______________________
- [ ] ______________________
- [ ] ______________________

WEEK 3: WTAG SCORE ____________

- [ ] ______________________
- [ ] ______________________
- [ ] ______________________
- [ ] ______________________

WEEK 4: WTAG SCORE ____________

- [ ] ______________________
- [ ] ______________________
- [ ] ______________________
- [ ] ______________________

WEEK 5: WTAG SCORE ____________

- [ ] ______________________
- [ ] ______________________
- [ ] ______________________
- [ ] ______________________

WEEKLY TEAM MEMBER

____

W.T.A.G. (WORKED TOWARD ANNUAL GOAL) SCORE 1- 10 BELOW ANNUAL GOAL: ______________

____

LIST & SCORE OPPORTUNITIES

WEEK 1: WTAG SCORE ______________

- [ ] ______________
- [ ] ______________
- [ ] ______________
- [ ] ______________

WEEK 2: WTAG SCORE ______________

- [ ] ______________
- [ ] ______________
- [ ] ______________
- [ ] ______________

WEEK 3: WTAG SCORE ______________

- [ ] ______________
- [ ] ______________
- [ ] ______________
- [ ] ______________

WEEK 4: WTAG SCORE ______________

- [ ] ______________
- [ ] ______________
- [ ] ______________
- [ ] ______________

WEEK 5: WTAG SCORE ______________

- [ ] ______________
- [ ] ______________
- [ ] ______________
- [ ] ______________

LIST & SCORE POSITIVES

WEEK 1: WTAG SCORE ______________

- [ ] ______________
- [ ] ______________
- [ ] ______________
- [ ] ______________

WEEK 2: WTAG SCORE ______________

- [ ] ______________
- [ ] ______________
- [ ] ______________
- [ ] ______________

WEEK 3: WTAG SCORE ______________

- [ ] ______________
- [ ] ______________
- [ ] ______________
- [ ] ______________

WEEK 4: WTAG SCORE ______________

- [ ] ______________
- [ ] ______________
- [ ] ______________
- [ ] ______________

WEEK 5: WTAG SCORE ______________

- [ ] ______________
- [ ] ______________
- [ ] ______________
- [ ] ______________

WEEKLY TEAM MEMBER

W.T.A.G. (WORKED TOWARD ANNUAL GOAL) SCORE 1- 10 BELOW ANNUAL GOAL:

LIST & SCORE OPPORTUNITIES

WEEK 1: WTAG SCORE

- [ ]
- [ ]
- [ ]
- [ ]

WEEK 2: WTAG SCORE

- [ ]
- [ ]
- [ ]
- [ ]

WEEK 3: WTAG SCORE

- [ ]
- [ ]
- [ ]
- [ ]

WEEK 4: WTAG SCORE

- [ ]
- [ ]
- [ ]
- [ ]

WEEK 5: WTAG SCORE

- [ ]
- [ ]
- [ ]
- [ ]

LIST & SCORE POSITIVES

WEEK 1: WTAG SCORE

- [ ]
- [ ]
- [ ]
- [ ]

WEEK 2: WTAG SCORE

- [ ]
- [ ]
- [ ]
- [ ]

WEEK 3: WTAG SCORE

- [ ]
- [ ]
- [ ]
- [ ]

WEEK 4: WTAG SCORE

- [ ]
- [ ]
- [ ]
- [ ]

WEEK 5: WTAG SCORE

- [ ]
- [ ]
- [ ]
- [ ]

Weekly Team Member

____

W.T.A.G. (WORKED TOWARD ANNUAL GOAL) SCORE 1- 10 BELOW ANNUAL GOAL: ______________

____

List & score opportunities

WEEK 1: WTAG SCORE ______________

- [ ] ______________
- [ ] ______________
- [ ] ______________
- [ ] ______________

WEEK 2: WTAG SCORE ______________

- [ ] ______________
- [ ] ______________
- [ ] ______________
- [ ] ______________

WEEK 3: WTAG SCORE ______________

- [ ] ______________
- [ ] ______________
- [ ] ______________
- [ ] ______________

WEEK 4: WTAG SCORE ______________

- [ ] ______________
- [ ] ______________
- [ ] ______________
- [ ] ______________

WEEK 5: WTAG SCORE ______________

- [ ] ______________
- [ ] ______________
- [ ] ______________
- [ ] ______________

List & score Positives

WEEK 1: WTAG SCORE ______________

- [ ] ______________
- [ ] ______________
- [ ] ______________
- [ ] ______________

WEEK 2: WTAG SCORE ______________

- [ ] ______________
- [ ] ______________
- [ ] ______________
- [ ] ______________

WEEK 3: WTAG SCORE ______________

- [ ] ______________
- [ ] ______________
- [ ] ______________
- [ ] ______________

WEEK 4: WTAG SCORE ______________

- [ ] ______________
- [ ] ______________
- [ ] ______________
- [ ] ______________

WEEK 5: WTAG SCORE ______________

- [ ] ______________
- [ ] ______________
- [ ] ______________
- [ ] ______________

WEEKLY TEAM MEMBER

W.T.A.G. (WORKED TOWARD ANNUAL GOAL) SCORE 1- 10 BELOW ANNUAL GOAL:

LIST & SCORE OPPORTUNITIES

WEEK 1: WTAG SCORE

- ☐
- ☐
- ☐
- ☐

WEEK 2: WTAG SCORE

- ☐
- ☐
- ☐
- ☐

WEEK 3: WTAG SCORE

- ☐
- ☐
- ☐
- ☐

WEEK 4: WTAG SCORE

- ☐
- ☐
- ☐
- ☐

WEEK 5: WTAG SCORE

- ☐
- ☐
- ☐
- ☐

LIST & SCORE POSITIVES

WEEK 1: WTAG SCORE

- ☐
- ☐
- ☐
- ☐

WEEK 2: WTAG SCORE

- ☐
- ☐
- ☐
- ☐

WEEK 3: WTAG SCORE

- ☐
- ☐
- ☐
- ☐

WEEK 4: WTAG SCORE

- ☐
- ☐
- ☐
- ☐

WEEK 5: WTAG SCORE

- ☐
- ☐
- ☐
- ☐

Weekly Team Member

W.T.A.G. (WORKED TOWARD ANNUAL GOAL) SCORE 1- 10 BELOW ANNUAL GOAL:

List & score Opportunities	List & score Positives
WEEK 1: WTAG SCORE	WEEK 1: WTAG SCORE
☐	☐
☐	☐
☐	☐
☐	☐
WEEK 2: WTAG SCORE	WEEK 2: WTAG SCORE
☐	☐
☐	☐
☐	☐
☐	☐
WEEK 3: WTAG SCORE	WEEK 3: WTAG SCORE
☐	☐
☐	☐
☐	☐
☐	☐
WEEK 4: WTAG SCORE	WEEK 4: WTAG SCORE
☐	☐
☐	☐
☐	☐
☐	☐
WEEK 5: WTAG SCORE	WEEK 5: WTAG SCORE
☐	☐
☐	☐
☐	☐
☐	☐

Weekly Team Member

____

W.T.A.G. (WORKED TOWARD ANNUAL GOAL) SCORE 1- 10 BELOW ANNUAL GOAL: _______________

____

List & score opportunities

WEEK 1: WTAG SCORE _______________

- [ ] _______________
- [ ] _______________
- [ ] _______________
- [ ] _______________

WEEK 2: WTAG SCORE _______________

- [ ] _______________
- [ ] _______________
- [ ] _______________
- [ ] _______________

WEEK 3: WTAG SCORE _______________

- [ ] _______________
- [ ] _______________
- [ ] _______________
- [ ] _______________

WEEK 4: WTAG SCORE _______________

- [ ] _______________
- [ ] _______________
- [ ] _______________
- [ ] _______________

WEEK 5: WTAG SCORE _______________

- [ ] _______________
- [ ] _______________
- [ ] _______________
- [ ] _______________

List & score Positives

WEEK 1: WTAG SCORE _______________

- [ ] _______________
- [ ] _______________
- [ ] _______________
- [ ] _______________

WEEK 2: WTAG SCORE _______________

- [ ] _______________
- [ ] _______________
- [ ] _______________
- [ ] _______________

WEEK 3: WTAG SCORE _______________

- [ ] _______________
- [ ] _______________
- [ ] _______________
- [ ] _______________

WEEK 4: WTAG SCORE _______________

- [ ] _______________
- [ ] _______________
- [ ] _______________
- [ ] _______________

WEEK 5: WTAG SCORE _______________

- [ ] _______________
- [ ] _______________
- [ ] _______________
- [ ] _______________

TEAM MEETING

WEEK: ____________

WINS/SUCCESSES

OPPORTUNITIES FOR IMPROVEMENT

PROJECTIONS & MONTHLY GOAL TRACKING

NEW PATIENTS: ____________

CAPTURE RATE: ____________

AVERAGE SALE: ____________

STAFF PRODUCTIVITY: ____________

WEEKLY CHECKLIST TO ACHIEVE MONTHLY GOAL

- ☐ ____________
- ☐ ____________
- ☐ ____________
- ☐ ____________

NOTES

DAILY PERSONAL PLANNER

DATE: ____________________ S M T W T F S

"I have not failed. I've just found 10,000 ways that won't work."
— Thomas Edison

TODAY'S SCHEDULE

6:00 ____________________
7:00 ____________________
8:00 ____________________
9:00 ____________________
10:00 ____________________
11:00 ____________________
12:00 ____________________
13:00 ____________________
14:00 ____________________
15:00 ____________________
16:00 ____________________
17:00 ____________________
18:00 ____________________
19:00 ____________________
20:00 ____________________
21:00 ____________________
22:00 ____________________

ACTION PLAN (TOP 3 PRIORITIES)

- ☐ ____________________
- ☐ ____________________
- ☐ ____________________

TASKS

- ☐ ____________________
- ☐ ____________________
- ☐ ____________________

WORK OUT COMPLETE

- ☐

WATER INTAKE

BREAKFAST PLAN ____________________

LUNCH PLAN ____________________

DINNER PLAN ____________________

HOURS SLEPT ____________________

END OF DAY REFLECTION: CELEBRATE TEAM MEMBERS & DAILY SUCCESS

____

____

END OF DAY REFLECTION: WHAT NEEDS IMPROVEMENT?

____

____

Daily Personal Planner

DATE: ____________________ S M T W T F S

"The key to successful leadership today is influence, not authority."
—Kenneth Blanchard

Today's Schedule

6:00 ______

7:00 ______

8:00 ______

9:00 ______

10:00 ______

11:00 ______

12:00 ______

13:00 ______

14:00 ______

15:00 ______

16:00 ______

17:00 ______

18:00 ______

19:00 ______

20:00 ______

21:00 ______

22:00 ______

Action Plan (Top 3 priorities)

- ☐ ______
- ☐ ______
- ☐ ______

TASKS

- ☐ ______
- ☐ ______
- ☐ ______

WORK OUT COMPLETE

☐

WATER INTAKE

Breakfast Plan ______

Lunch Plan ______

Dinner Plan ______

Hours Slept ______

End of Day Reflection: Celebrate Team members & Daily success

______

______

End of Day Reflection: what needs improvement?

______

______

Daily Personal Planner

DATE: ____________________ S M T W T F S

"Don't be intimidated by what you don't know. That can be your greatest strength and ensure that you do things differently from everyone else." — Sara Blakely

Today's Schedule

6:00

7:00

8:00

9:00

10:00

11:00

12:00

13:00

14:00

15:00

16:00

17:00

18:00

19:00

20:00

21:00

22:00

Action Plan (Top 3 priorities)

- ☐
- ☐
- ☐

TASKS

- ☐
- ☐
- ☐

WORK OUT COMPLETE

- ☐

WATER INTAKE

Breakfast Plan

Lunch Plan

Dinner Plan

Hours Slept

End of Day Reflection: Celebrate Team members & Daily success

End of Day Reflection: what needs improvement?

DAILY PERSONAL PLANNER

DATE: ______________ S M T W T F S

"The price of success is hard work, dedication to the job at hand, and the determination that whether we win or lose, we have applied the best of ourselves to the task at hand."
— Vince Lombardi

TODAY'S SCHEDULE

6:00
7:00
8:00
9:00
10:00
11:00
12:00
13:00
14:00
15:00
16:00
17:00
18:00
19:00
20:00
21:00
22:00

ACTION PLAN (TOP 3 PRIORITIES)

- [ ]
- [ ]
- [ ]

TASKS

- [ ]
- [ ]
- [ ]

WORK OUT COMPLETE

- [ ]

WATER INTAKE

BREAKFAST PLAN ______________

LUNCH PLAN ______________

DINNER PLAN ______________

HOURS SLEPT ______________

END OF DAY REFLECTION: CELEBRATE TEAM MEMBERS & DAILY SUCCESS

END OF DAY REFLECTION: WHAT NEEDS IMPROVEMENT?

DAILY PERSONAL PLANNER

DATE: ______________________ S M T W T F S

"The future belongs to those who believe in the beauty of their dreams."
— Eleanor Roosevelt

TODAY'S SCHEDULE

6:00 ____
7:00 ____
8:00 ____
9:00 ____
10:00 ____
11:00 ____
12:00 ____
13:00 ____
14:00 ____
15:00 ____
16:00 ____
17:00 ____
18:00 ____
19:00 ____
20:00 ____
21:00 ____
22:00 ____

ACTION PLAN (TOP 3 PRIORITIES)

- ☐ ____
- ☐ ____
- ☐ ____

TASKS

- ☐ ____
- ☐ ____
- ☐ ____

WORK OUT COMPLETE

- ☐

WATER INTAKE

BREAKFAST PLAN ____

LUNCH PLAN ____

DINNER PLAN ____

HOURS SLEPT ____

END OF DAY REFLECTION: CELEBRATE TEAM MEMBERS & DAILY SUCCESS

____

____

END OF DAY REFLECTION: WHAT NEEDS IMPROVEMENT?

____

____

DAILY PERSONAL PLANNER

DATE: ______________________ S M T W T F S

"The secret of getting ahead is getting started."
— Mark Twain

TODAY'S SCHEDULE

6:00
7:00
8:00
9:00
10:00
11:00
12:00
13:00
14:00
15:00
16:00
17:00
18:00
19:00
20:00
21:00
22:00

ACTION PLAN (TOP 3 PRIORITIES)

- ☐
- ☐
- ☐

TASKS

- ☐
- ☐
- ☐

WORK OUT COMPLETE

- ☐

WATER INTAKE

BREAKFAST PLAN ______________________

LUNCH PLAN ______________________

DINNER PLAN ______________________

HOURS SLEPT ______________________

END OF DAY REFLECTION: CELEBRATE TEAM MEMBERS & DAILY SUCCESS

END OF DAY REFLECTION: WHAT NEEDS IMPROVEMENT?

Daily Personal Planner

DATE: ______________________ S M T W T F S

"Success is not final; failure is not fatal: It is the courage to continue that counts."
— Winston Churchill

TODAY'S SCHEDULE

6:00
7:00
8:00
9:00
10:00
11:00
12:00
13:00
14:00
15:00
16:00
17:00
18:00
19:00
20:00
21:00
22:00

ACTION PLAN (TOP 3 PRIORITIES)

- ☐
- ☐
- ☐

TASKS

- ☐
- ☐
- ☐

WORK OUT COMPLETE

☐

WATER INTAKE

BREAKFAST PLAN

LUNCH PLAN

DINNER PLAN

HOURS SLEPT

END OF DAY REFLECTION: CELEBRATE TEAM MEMBERS & DAILY SUCCESS

END OF DAY REFLECTION: WHAT NEEDS IMPROVEMENT?

TEAM MEETING

WEEK: ____________

WINS/SUCCESSES

OPPORTUNITIES FOR IMPROVEMENT

PROJECTIONS & MONTHLY GOAL TRACKING

NEW PATIENTS: ____________

CAPTURE RATE: ____________

AVERAGE SALE: ____________

STAFF PRODUCTIVITY: ____________

WEEKLY CHECKLIST TO ACHIEVE MONTHLY GOAL

- ☐ ____________
- ☐ ____________
- ☐ ____________
- ☐ ____________

NOTES

DAILY PERSONAL PLANNER

DATE: ____________________ S M T W T F S

"Successful entrepreneurs know that the best way to predict the future is to create it."
— Peter Drucker

TODAY'S SCHEDULE

6:00 ____________________
7:00 ____________________
8:00 ____________________
9:00 ____________________
10:00 ____________________
11:00 ____________________
12:00 ____________________
13:00 ____________________
14:00 ____________________
15:00 ____________________
16:00 ____________________
17:00 ____________________
18:00 ____________________
19:00 ____________________
20:00 ____________________
21:00 ____________________
22:00 ____________________

ACTION PLAN (TOP 3 PRIORITIES)

- [ ] ____________________
- [ ] ____________________
- [ ] ____________________

TASKS

- [ ] ____________________
- [ ] ____________________
- [ ] ____________________

WORK OUT COMPLETE

- [ ]

WATER INTAKE

BREAKFAST PLAN ____________________

LUNCH PLAN ____________________

DINNER PLAN ____________________

HOURS SLEPT ____________________

END OF DAY REFLECTION: CELEBRATE TEAM MEMBERS & DAILY SUCCESS

____

____

END OF DAY REFLECTION: WHAT NEEDS IMPROVEMENT?

____

____

Daily Personal Planner

DATE: ____________________ S M T W T F S

"If you don't build your dream, someone else will hire you to help them build theirs."
— Dhirubhai Ambani

Today's Schedule

6:00 ____________________
7:00 ____________________
8:00 ____________________
9:00 ____________________
10:00 ____________________
11:00 ____________________
12:00 ____________________
13:00 ____________________
14:00 ____________________
15:00 ____________________
16:00 ____________________
17:00 ____________________
18:00 ____________________
19:00 ____________________
20:00 ____________________
21:00 ____________________
22:00 ____________________

Action Plan (Top 3 priorities)

- ☐ ____________________
- ☐ ____________________
- ☐ ____________________

Tasks

- ☐ ____________________
- ☐ ____________________
- ☐ ____________________

Work out complete

- ☐

Water intake

Breakfast Plan ____________________

Lunch Plan ____________________

Dinner Plan ____________________

Hours Slept ____________________

End of Day Reflection: Celebrate Team members & Daily success

____

____

End of Day Reflection: what needs improvement?

____

____

DAILY PERSONAL PLANNER

DATE: ____________________   S M T W T F S

"The successful warrior is the average man, with laser-like focus."
— Bruce Lee

TODAY'S SCHEDULE

6:00

7:00

8:00

9:00

10:00

11:00

12:00

13:00

14:00

15:00

16:00

17:00

18:00

19:00

20:00

21:00

22:00

ACTION PLAN (TOP 3 PRIORITIES)

- ☐
- ☐
- ☐

TASKS

- ☐
- ☐
- ☐

WORK OUT COMPLETE

- ☐

WATER INTAKE

BREAKFAST PLAN

LUNCH PLAN

DINNER PLAN

HOURS SLEPT

END OF DAY REFLECTION: CELEBRATE TEAM MEMBERS & DAILY SUCCESS

END OF DAY REFLECTION: WHAT NEEDS IMPROVEMENT?

Daily Personal Planner

DATE: ____________________ S M T W T F S

"The secret of success is to do the common things uncommonly well."
— John D. Rockefeller

Today's Schedule

6:00 ____________________
7:00 ____________________
8:00 ____________________
9:00 ____________________
10:00 ____________________
11:00 ____________________
12:00 ____________________
13:00 ____________________
14:00 ____________________
15:00 ____________________
16:00 ____________________
17:00 ____________________
18:00 ____________________
19:00 ____________________
20:00 ____________________
21:00 ____________________
22:00 ____________________

Action Plan (Top 3 priorities)

- ☐ ____________________
- ☐ ____________________
- ☐ ____________________

Tasks

- ☐ ____________________
- ☐ ____________________
- ☐ ____________________

Work Out Complete

- ☐

Water Intake

Breakfast Plan ____________________

Lunch Plan ____________________

Dinner Plan ____________________

Hours Slept ____________________

End of Day Reflection: Celebrate Team members & Daily success

____

____

End of Day Reflection: what needs improvement?

____

____

Daily Personal Planner

DATE: ____________________ S M T W T F S

"Successful people do what unsuccessful people are not willing to do. Don't wish it were easier; wish you were better." — Jim Rohn

Today's Schedule

6:00
7:00
8:00
9:00
10:00
11:00
12:00
13:00
14:00
15:00
16:00
17:00
18:00
19:00
20:00
21:00
22:00

Action Plan (Top 3 priorities)

- [ ]
- [ ]
- [ ]

TASKS

- [ ]
- [ ]
- [ ]

WORK OUT COMPLETE

- [ ]

WATER INTAKE

Breakfast Plan ____________________

Lunch Plan ____________________

Dinner Plan ____________________

Hours Slept ____________________

End of Day Reflection: Celebrate Team members & Daily success

End of Day Reflection: what needs improvement?

DAILY PERSONAL PLANNER

DATE: ____________________ S M T W T F S

"The most successful people are those who excel in the face of adversity."
— Unknown

TODAY'S SCHEDULE

6:00

7:00

8:00

9:00

10:00

11:00

12:00

13:00

14:00

15:00

16:00

17:00

18:00

19:00

20:00

21:00

22:00

ACTION PLAN (TOP 3 PRIORITIES)

- ☐
- ☐
- ☐

TASKS

- ☐
- ☐
- ☐

WORK OUT COMPLETE

- ☐

WATER INTAKE

BREAKFAST PLAN

LUNCH PLAN

DINNER PLAN

HOURS SLEPT

END OF DAY REFLECTION: CELEBRATE TEAM MEMBERS & DAILY SUCCESS

END OF DAY REFLECTION: WHAT NEEDS IMPROVEMENT?

DAILY PERSONAL PLANNER

DATE: ____________ S M T W T F S

"The biggest risk is not taking any risk. In a world that's changing quickly, the only strategy that is guaranteed to fail is not taking risks." - Mark Zuckerberg

TODAY'S SCHEDULE

6:00
7:00
8:00
9:00
10:00
11:00
12:00
13:00
14:00
15:00
16:00
17:00
18:00
19:00
20:00
21:00
22:00

ACTION PLAN (TOP 3 PRIORITIES)

- [ ]
- [ ]
- [ ]

TASKS

- [ ]
- [ ]
- [ ]

WORK OUT COMPLETE

- [ ]

WATER INTAKE

BREAKFAST PLAN

LUNCH PLAN

DINNER PLAN

HOURS SLEPT

END OF DAY REFLECTION: CELEBRATE TEAM MEMBERS & DAILY SUCCESS

END OF DAY REFLECTION: WHAT NEEDS IMPROVEMENT?

Team Meeting

Week: ____________

WINS/SUCCESSES

OPPORTUNITIES FOR IMPROVEMENT

Projections & Monthly Goal Tracking

New Patients: ____________

Capture Rate: ____________

Average Sale: ____________

Staff Productivity: ____________

Weekly Checklist to Achieve Monthly Goal

- [ ]
- [ ]
- [ ]
- [ ]

NOTES

Daily Personal Planner

Date: ____________________ S M T W T F S

"The biggest adventure you can ever take is to live the life of your dreams."
- Oprah Winfrey

Today's Schedule

6:00 ____________________
7:00 ____________________
8:00 ____________________
9:00 ____________________
10:00 ____________________
11:00 ____________________
12:00 ____________________
13:00 ____________________
14:00 ____________________
15:00 ____________________
16:00 ____________________
17:00 ____________________
18:00 ____________________
19:00 ____________________
20:00 ____________________
21:00 ____________________
22:00 ____________________

Action Plan (Top 3 priorities)

- [ ] ____________________
- [ ] ____________________
- [ ] ____________________

Tasks

- [ ] ____________________
- [ ] ____________________
- [ ] ____________________

Work out complete

- [ ]

Water intake

Breakfast Plan ____________________

Lunch Plan ____________________

Dinner Plan ____________________

Hours Slept ____________________

End of Day Reflection: Celebrate Team members & Daily success

____

____

End of Day Reflection: what needs improvement?

____

____

Daily Personal Planner

DATE: ____________________ S M T W T F S

"Success is not the key to happiness. Happiness is the key to success. If you love what you are doing, you will be successful." - Albert Schweitzer

Today's Schedule

6:00

7:00

8:00

9:00

10:00

11:00

12:00

13:00

14:00

15:00

16:00

17:00

18:00

19:00

20:00

21:00

22:00

Action Plan (Top 3 priorities)

- ☐
- ☐
- ☐

TASKS

- ☐
- ☐
- ☐

WORK OUT COMPLETE

- ☐

WATER INTAKE

Breakfast Plan

Lunch Plan

Dinner Plan

Hours Slept

End of Day Reflection: Celebrate Team members & Daily success

End of Day Reflection: what needs improvement?

Daily Personal Planner

DATE: ______________________ S M T W T F S

"The only limit to our realization of tomorrow will be our doubts of today."
- Franklin D. Roosevelt

Today's Schedule

6:00
7:00
8:00
9:00
10:00
11:00
12:00
13:00
14:00
15:00
16:00
17:00
18:00
19:00
20:00
21:00
22:00

Action Plan (Top 3 priorities)

- ☐
- ☐
- ☐

TASKS

- ☐
- ☐
- ☐

WORK OUT COMPLETE

- ☐

WATER INTAKE

Breakfast Plan

Lunch Plan

Dinner Plan

Hours Slept

End of Day Reflection: Celebrate Team members & Daily success

End of Day Reflection: what needs improvement?

Daily Personal Planner

DATE: ______________________ S M T W T F S

"You miss 100% of the shots you don't take."
- Wayne Gretzky

Today's Schedule

6:00 ____________________
7:00 ____________________
8:00 ____________________
9:00 ____________________
10:00 ____________________
11:00 ____________________
12:00 ____________________
13:00 ____________________
14:00 ____________________
15:00 ____________________
16:00 ____________________
17:00 ____________________
18:00 ____________________
19:00 ____________________
20:00 ____________________
21:00 ____________________
22:00 ____________________

Action Plan (Top 3 priorities)

- ☐ ____________________
- ☐ ____________________
- ☐ ____________________

TASKS

- ☐ ____________________
- ☐ ____________________
- ☐ ____________________

WORK OUT COMPLETE

- ☐

WATER INTAKE

Breakfast Plan ____________________

Lunch Plan ____________________

Dinner Plan ____________________

Hours Slept ____________________

End of Day Reflection: Celebrate Team members & Daily success

____

____

End of Day Reflection: what needs improvement?

____

____

DAILY PERSONAL PLANNER

DATE: ______________________ S M T W T F S

"The best way to find yourself is to lose yourself in the service of others."
- Mahatma Gandhi

TODAY'S SCHEDULE

6:00

7:00

8:00

9:00

10:00

11:00

12:00

13:00

14:00

15:00

16:00

17:00

18:00

19:00

20:00

21:00

22:00

ACTION PLAN (TOP 3 PRIORITIES)

- ☐
- ☐
- ☐

TASKS

- ☐
- ☐
- ☐

WORK OUT COMPLETE

- ☐

WATER INTAKE

BREAKFAST PLAN

LUNCH PLAN

DINNER PLAN

HOURS SLEPT

END OF DAY REFLECTION: CELEBRATE TEAM MEMBERS & DAILY SUCCESS

END OF DAY REFLECTION: WHAT NEEDS IMPROVEMENT?

DAILY PERSONAL PLANNER

DATE: ______________________ S M T W T F S

"The only way to do great work is to love what you do. If you haven't found it yet, keep looking. Don't settle. As with all matters of the heart, you'll know when you find it."
- Steve Jobs

TODAY'S SCHEDULE

6:00

7:00

8:00

9:00

10:00

11:00

12:00

13:00

14:00

15:00

16:00

17:00

18:00

19:00

20:00

21:00

22:00

ACTION PLAN (TOP 3 PRIORITIES)

- ☐
- ☐
- ☐

TASKS

- ☐
- ☐
- ☐

WORK OUT COMPLETE

- ☐

WATER INTAKE

BREAKFAST PLAN

LUNCH PLAN

DINNER PLAN

HOURS SLEPT

END OF DAY REFLECTION: CELEBRATE TEAM MEMBERS & DAILY SUCCESS

END OF DAY REFLECTION: WHAT NEEDS IMPROVEMENT?

Daily Personal Planner

Date: ______________________ S M T W T F S

"The best time to plant a tree was 20 years ago. The second best time is now."
- Chinese Proverb

Today's Schedule

6:00 ____
7:00 ____
8:00 ____
9:00 ____
10:00 ____
11:00 ____
12:00 ____
13:00 ____
14:00 ____
15:00 ____
16:00 ____
17:00 ____
18:00 ____
19:00 ____
20:00 ____
21:00 ____
22:00 ____

Action Plan (Top 3 priorities)

- ☐ ____
- ☐ ____
- ☐ ____

TASKS

- ☐ ____
- ☐ ____
- ☐ ____

WORK OUT COMPLETE

- ☐

WATER INTAKE

Breakfast Plan ____

Lunch Plan ____

Dinner Plan ____

Hours Slept ____

End of Day Reflection: Celebrate Team members & Daily success

____

____

End of Day Reflection: what needs improvement?

____

____

Team Meeting

Week: ____________

WINS/SUCCESSES

OPPORTUNITIES FOR IMPROVEMENT

Projections & Monthly Goal Tracking

New Patients: ____________

Capture Rate: ____________

Average Sale: ____________

Staff Productivity: ____________

Weekly Checklist to Achieve Monthly Goal

- [ ] ____________
- [ ] ____________
- [ ] ____________
- [ ] ____________

Notes

Daily Personal Planner

DATE: ______________________ S M T W T F S

"You can't build a reputation on what you are going to do."
- Henry Ford

Today's Schedule

6:00 ____
7:00 ____
8:00 ____
9:00 ____
10:00 ____
11:00 ____
12:00 ____
13:00 ____
14:00 ____
15:00 ____
16:00 ____
17:00 ____
18:00 ____
19:00 ____
20:00 ____
21:00 ____
22:00 ____

Action Plan (Top 3 priorities)

- ☐ ____
- ☐ ____
- ☐ ____

TASKS

- ☐ ____
- ☐ ____
- ☐ ____

WORK OUT COMPLETE

☐

WATER INTAKE

Breakfast Plan ____

Lunch Plan ____

Dinner Plan ____

Hours Slept ____

End of Day Reflection: Celebrate Team members & Daily success

____

____

End of Day Reflection: what needs improvement?

____

____

DAILY PERSONAL PLANNER

DATE: ____________________ S M T W T F S

"Your most unhappy patient is your greatest source of learning"
- Bill Gates

TODAY'S SCHEDULE

6:00
7:00
8:00
9:00
10:00
11:00
12:00
13:00
14:00
15:00
16:00
17:00
18:00
19:00
20:00
21:00
22:00

ACTION PLAN (TOP 3 PRIORITIES)

- ☐
- ☐
- ☐

TASKS

- ☐
- ☐
- ☐

WORK OUT COMPLETE

- ☐

WATER INTAKE

BREAKFAST PLAN

LUNCH PLAN

DINNER PLAN

HOURS SLEPT

END OF DAY REFLECTION: CELEBRATE TEAM MEMBERS & DAILY SUCCESS

END OF DAY REFLECTION: WHAT NEEDS IMPROVEMENT?

Daily Personal Planner

DATE: ______________________ S M T W T F S

"Success is not final, failure is not fatal: It is the courage to continue that counts."
- Winston Churchill

Today's Schedule

6:00 ______
7:00 ______
8:00 ______
9:00 ______
10:00 ______
11:00 ______
12:00 ______
13:00 ______
14:00 ______
15:00 ______
16:00 ______
17:00 ______
18:00 ______
19:00 ______
20:00 ______
21:00 ______
22:00 ______

Action Plan (Top 3 priorities)

- ☐ ______
- ☐ ______
- ☐ ______

TASKS

- ☐ ______
- ☐ ______
- ☐ ______

WORK OUT COMPLETE

- ☐

WATER INTAKE

Breakfast Plan ______

Lunch Plan ______

Dinner Plan ______

Hours Slept ______

End of Day Reflection: Celebrate Team members & Daily success

______

______

End of Day Reflection: what needs improvement?

______

______

DAILY PERSONAL PLANNER

DATE: ____________________ S M T W T F S

• *"The road to success and greatness is always paved with consistent hard work. Outwork your competitors and be relentless." – Unknown*

TODAY'S SCHEDULE

6:00 ____________________

7:00 ____________________

8:00 ____________________

9:00 ____________________

10:00 ____________________

11:00 ____________________

12:00 ____________________

13:00 ____________________

14:00 ____________________

15:00 ____________________

16:00 ____________________

17:00 ____________________

18:00 ____________________

19:00 ____________________

20:00 ____________________

21:00 ____________________

22:00 ____________________

ACTION PLAN (TOP 3 PRIORITIES)

- ☐ ____________________
- ☐ ____________________
- ☐ ____________________

TASKS

- ☐ ____________________
- ☐ ____________________
- ☐ ____________________

WORK OUT COMPLETE

☐

WATER INTAKE

BREAKFAST PLAN ____________________

LUNCH PLAN ____________________

DINNER PLAN ____________________

HOURS SLEPT ____________________

END OF DAY REFLECTION: CELEBRATE TEAM MEMBERS & DAILY SUCCESS

____

____

END OF DAY REFLECTION: WHAT NEEDS IMPROVEMENT?

____

____

DAILY PERSONAL PLANNER

DATE: ______________________ S M T W T F S

"Successful people do what unsuccessful people are not willing to do. Don't wish it were easier, wish you were better." – Jim Rohn

TODAY'S SCHEDULE

6:00

7:00

8:00

9:00

10:00

11:00

12:00

13:00

14:00

15:00

16:00

17:00

18:00

19:00

20:00

21:00

22:00

ACTION PLAN (TOP 3 PRIORITIES)

- ☐
- ☐
- ☐

TASKS

- ☐
- ☐
- ☐

WORK OUT COMPLETE

☐

WATER INTAKE

BREAKFAST PLAN

LUNCH PLAN

DINNER PLAN

HOURS SLEPT

END OF DAY REFLECTION: CELEBRATE TEAM MEMBERS & DAILY SUCCESS

END OF DAY REFLECTION: WHAT NEEDS IMPROVEMENT?

DAILY PERSONAL PLANNER

DATE: ____________________ S M T W T F S

•"The best way to predict the future is to create it."
–Peter Drucker

TODAY'S SCHEDULE

6:00
7:00
8:00
9:00
10:00
11:00
12:00
13:00
14:00
15:00
16:00
17:00
18:00
19:00
20:00
21:00
22:00

ACTION PLAN (TOP 3 PRIORITIES)

- ☐
- ☐
- ☐

TASKS

- ☐
- ☐
- ☐

WORK OUT COMPLETE

- ☐

WATER INTAKE

BREAKFAST PLAN ____________

LUNCH PLAN ____________

DINNER PLAN ____________

HOURS SLEPT ____________

END OF DAY REFLECTION: CELEBRATE TEAM MEMBERS & DAILY SUCCESS

END OF DAY REFLECTION: WHAT NEEDS IMPROVEMENT?

DAILY PERSONAL PLANNER

DATE: ____________________ S M T W T F S

"You don't have to be great to start, but you have to start to be great."
–Zig Ziglar

TODAY'S SCHEDULE

6:00
7:00
8:00
9:00
10:00
11:00
12:00
13:00
14:00
15:00
16:00
17:00
18:00
19:00
20:00
21:00
22:00

ACTION PLAN (TOP 3 PRIORITIES)

- ☐
- ☐
- ☐

TASKS

- ☐
- ☐
- ☐

WORK OUT COMPLETE

☐

WATER INTAKE

BREAKFAST PLAN

LUNCH PLAN

DINNER PLAN

HOURS SLEPT

END OF DAY REFLECTION: CELEBRATE TEAM MEMBERS & DAILY SUCCESS

END OF DAY REFLECTION: WHAT NEEDS IMPROVEMENT?

Team Meeting

Week: ______________

WINS/SUCCESSES

OPPORTUNITIES FOR IMPROVEMENT

Projections & Monthly Goal Tracking

New Patients: ______________

Capture Rate: ______________

Average Sale: ______________

Staff Productivity: ______________

Weekly Checklist to Achieve Monthly Goal

- ☐ ______________
- ☐ ______________
- ☐ ______________
- ☐ ______________

Notes

Daily Personal Planner

DATE: ______________________ S M T W T F S

"Success is walking from failure to failure with no loss of enthusiasm."
– Winston Churchill

Today's Schedule

6:00 ____________________

7:00 ____________________

8:00 ____________________

9:00 ____________________

10:00 ____________________

11:00 ____________________

12:00 ____________________

13:00 ____________________

14:00 ____________________

15:00 ____________________

16:00 ____________________

17:00 ____________________

18:00 ____________________

19:00 ____________________

20:00 ____________________

21:00 ____________________

22:00 ____________________

Action Plan (Top 3 priorities)

- [ ] ____________________
- [ ] ____________________
- [ ] ____________________

Tasks

- [ ] ____________________
- [ ] ____________________
- [ ] ____________________

Work out complete

- [ ]

Water intake

Breakfast Plan ____________________

Lunch Plan ____________________

Dinner Plan ____________________

Hours Slept ____________________

End of Day Reflection: Celebrate Team members & Daily success

____

____

End of Day Reflection: what needs improvement?

____

____

Daily Personal Planner

DATE: ______________________ S M T W T F S

"Don't be afraid to give up the good to go for the great."
– John D. Rockefeller

Today's Schedule

6:00

7:00

8:00

9:00

10:00

11:00

12:00

13:00

14:00

15:00

16:00

17:00

18:00

19:00

20:00

21:00

22:00

Action Plan (Top 3 priorities)

- ☐
- ☐
- ☐

TASKS

- ☐
- ☐
- ☐

WORK OUT COMPLETE

- ☐

WATER INTAKE

Breakfast Plan ______________________

Lunch Plan ______________________

Dinner Plan ______________________

Hours Slept ______________________

End of Day Reflection: Celebrate Team members & Daily success

End of Day Reflection: what needs improvement?

Daily Personal Planner

DATE: ____________________ S M T W T F S

"Success is not the key to happiness. Happiness is the key to success. If you love what you are doing, you will be successful." – Albert Schweitzer

Today's Schedule

6:00

7:00

8:00

9:00

10:00

11:00

12:00

13:00

14:00

15:00

16:00

17:00

18:00

19:00

20:00

21:00

22:00

Action Plan (Top 3 priorities)

- ☐
- ☐
- ☐

TASKS

- ☐
- ☐
- ☐

WORK OUT COMPLETE

- ☐

WATER INTAKE

Breakfast Plan ____________________

Lunch Plan ____________________

Dinner Plan ____________________

Hours Slept ____________________

End of Day Reflection: Celebrate Team members & Daily success

End of Day Reflection: what needs improvement?

Daily Personal Planner

DATE: ______________________ S M T W T F S

"The most difficult thing is the decision to act, the rest is merely tenacity."
– Amelia Earhart

TODAY'S SCHEDULE

6:00
7:00
8:00
9:00
10:00
11:00
12:00
13:00
14:00
15:00
16:00
17:00
18:00
19:00
20:00
21:00
22:00

ACTION PLAN (TOP 3 PRIORITIES)

- ☐
- ☐
- ☐

TASKS

- ☐
- ☐
- ☐

WORK OUT COMPLETE

☐

WATER INTAKE

BREAKFAST PLAN

LUNCH PLAN

DINNER PLAN

HOURS SLEPT

END OF DAY REFLECTION: CELEBRATE TEAM MEMBERS & DAILY SUCCESS

END OF DAY REFLECTION: WHAT NEEDS IMPROVEMENT?

DAILY PERSONAL PLANNER

DATE: ____________________ S M T W T F S

"If you do what you've always done, you'll get what you've always gotten."
— Tony Robbins

TODAY'S SCHEDULE

6:00 ____
7:00 ____
8:00 ____
9:00 ____
10:00 ____
11:00 ____
12:00 ____
13:00 ____
14:00 ____
15:00 ____
16:00 ____
17:00 ____
18:00 ____
19:00 ____
20:00 ____
21:00 ____
22:00 ____

ACTION PLAN (TOP 3 PRIORITIES)

- ☐ ____
- ☐ ____
- ☐ ____

TASKS

- ☐ ____
- ☐ ____
- ☐ ____

WORK OUT COMPLETE

- ☐

WATER INTAKE

BREAKFAST PLAN ____

LUNCH PLAN ____

DINNER PLAN ____

HOURS SLEPT ____

END OF DAY REFLECTION: CELEBRATE TEAM MEMBERS & DAILY SUCCESS

____

____

END OF DAY REFLECTION: WHAT NEEDS IMPROVEMENT?

____

____

DAILY PERSONAL PLANNER

DATE: ____________________ S M T W T F S

"Be undeniably good. No marketing effort or social media buzzword can be a substitute for that." — Anthony Volodkin

TODAY'S SCHEDULE

6:00

7:00

8:00

9:00

10:00

11:00

12:00

13:00

14:00

15:00

16:00

17:00

18:00

19:00

20:00

21:00

22:00

ACTION PLAN (TOP 3 PRIORITIES)

- ☐
- ☐
- ☐

TASKS

- ☐
- ☐
- ☐

WORK OUT COMPLETE

☐

WATER INTAKE

BREAKFAST PLAN

LUNCH PLAN

DINNER PLAN

HOURS SLEPT

END OF DAY REFLECTION: CELEBRATE TEAM MEMBERS & DAILY SUCCESS

END OF DAY REFLECTION: WHAT NEEDS IMPROVEMENT?

DAILY PERSONAL PLANNER

DATE: ______________________ S M T W T F S

"You don't learn to walk by following rules. You learn by doing and falling over."
— Richard Branson

TODAY'S SCHEDULE

6:00
7:00
8:00
9:00
10:00
11:00
12:00
13:00
14:00
15:00
16:00
17:00
18:00
19:00
20:00
21:00
22:00

ACTION PLAN (TOP 3 PRIORITIES)

- ☐
- ☐
- ☐

TASKS

- ☐
- ☐
- ☐

WORK OUT COMPLETE

- ☐

WATER INTAKE

BREAKFAST PLAN ______________________

LUNCH PLAN ______________________

DINNER PLAN ______________________

HOURS SLEPT ______________________

END OF DAY REFLECTION: CELEBRATE TEAM MEMBERS & DAILY SUCCESS

END OF DAY REFLECTION: WHAT NEEDS IMPROVEMENT?

MONTH:

SUN	MON	TUES	WED	THUR	FRI	SAT

MONTH GOALS

1. ______________________________

2. ______________________________

3. ______________________________

TO DO LIST

- ☐
- ☐
- ☐
- ☐
- ☐

MONTHLY PRACTICE MANAGEMENT

SHORT TERM **MONTH 1:** **MONTH 2:** **MONTH 3:**

● SATISFIED ⊙ OKAY ⊗ DISSATISFIED

1	2	3	4	5	6	7
8	9	10	11	12	13	14
15	16	17	18	19	20	21
22	23	24	25	26	27	28
29	30	31				

MONTHLY FINDINGS

Monthly Marketing One-Sheet

"By Failing to prepare, you are preparing to fail." –Benjamin Franklin

Concept & Initiation (What)
Name: ______________________
Goal: ______________________
Estimated Timeline: ______________________
Targets to Reach: ______________________

Define & Plan: (How)
Budget: ______________________

List requirements: ______________________

Materials Needed: ______________________

Actions Needed: ______________________

Launch & Execution: (Who, When & Where)
Project Manager: ______________________

Define Details needed for each action: ______________________

Create Plan To Execute: ______________________

Performance & Control
Plan Details in Timeline: ______________________

Communication Plan Used: ______________________

Measuring Success: ______________________

Project Close
Training Needed: ______________________

Implementation Process: ______________________

Assessment of Success

Benchmarks: Professional

	Production YTD	Collections YTD	Net
Week 1			
Week 2			
Week 3			
Week 4			
Week 5			

KEY
YTD: Year to Date
M: Month
Ins. Coll: Insurance Collections
PT. Coll: Patient Collections
NP EX.: New Patient Exams
EP EX.: Established Patient
Exams
Total EX.: Total Exams
Prod. EX.: Production Per Exam
Coll. EX.: Collection Per Exam
Prof. Fees: Professional Fees

M	Ins. Coll.	Pt. Coll.	NP Ex.	EP Ex.	Total Ex.	Pro/ Ex.	Coll/ Ex.	Prof. Fees	Other	Other	Other
1											
2											
3											
4											
5											
6											
7											
8											
9											
10											
11											
12											

BENCHMARKS: RETAIL

	PRODUCTION YTD	COLLECTIONS YTD	NET
WEEK 1			
WEEK 2			
WEEK 3			
WEEK 4			
WEEK 5			

KEY
YTD: Year to Date
M: Month
Ins. Coll: Insurance Collections
PT. Coll: Patient Collections
# of Frames: Number of Frames
Fr. Coll.: Frames Collected
Ave Fr Sale: Average Frame Sale
Lens Sold: Number of Lens Sold
Fr. Coll.: Frames Collected
Ave. Lens Sale: Average Lens Sale
Cap. Rate: Capture Rate
CL Fit Eval: Total Contact Lens Fits
CL Yr Supp: Contact Lens Year Supply
CL Capt. Rate: Contact Lens Capture Rate
CL Coll: Contact Lens Collections
CL$/Fit: Average Contact Lens Sale/Fitting

M	INS. COLL.	PT. COLL.	# OF FRAMES	FR COLL.	AVE FR SALE	# LENS SOLD	FR COLL	AVE LENS SALE	CAP. RATE	CL FIT/ EVAL	CL YR SUPP	CL CAPT RATE	CL COLL	CL$ /FIT
1														
2														
3														
4														
5														
6														
7														
8														
9														
10														
11														
12														

Benchmarks: Special

	Production YTD	Collections YTD	Net
Week 1			
Week 2			
Week 3			
Week 4			
Week 5			

KEY
YTD: Year to Date
M: Month
Ins. Coll: Insurance Collections
PT. Coll: Patient Collections
VT Eval: Vision Therapy Evaluations
VT Conf: Vision Therapy Conferences
VT Sign-ups: Vision Therapy Sign-up
VT NS Rate: Vision Therapy No-show Rate
DE Eval: Vision Therapy Evaluations
DE Conf: Vision Therapy Conferences
DE Sign-ups: Vision Therapy Sign-up
CL Fit
CL Start: Contact Lens Starts
MD Eval: Macular Degeneration Evaluation
GL Eval: Glaucoma Evaluation
LV Eval: Low Vision Evaluation

M	Ins. Coll.	Pt. Coll.	VT Evals	VT Conf	VT Start	VT NS Rate	DE Eval	DE Conf	DE Start	CL Eval	MD Eval	GL Eval	LV Eval	Other
1														
2														
3														
4														
5														
6														
7														
8														
9														
10														
11														
12														

BENCHMARKS

INCOME

INCOME 1	
INCOME 2	
OTHER INCOME	
TOTAL	

EXPENSES

MONTH

BUDGET

TO BE PAID	DUE DATE	AMOUNT	PAID	NOTES

SUMMARY

TOTAL INCOME	TOTAL EXPENSES	DIFFERENCE

NOTES

Weekly Team Member

W.T.A.G. (WORKED TOWARD ANNUAL GOAL) SCORE 1- 10 BELOW ANNUAL GOAL:

List & score opportunities

WEEK 1: WTAG SCORE

- ☐
- ☐
- ☐
- ☐

WEEK 2: WTAG SCORE

- ☐
- ☐
- ☐
- ☐

WEEK 3: WTAG SCORE

- ☐
- ☐
- ☐
- ☐

WEEK 4: WTAG SCORE

- ☐
- ☐
- ☐
- ☐

WEEK 5: WTAG SCORE

- ☐
- ☐
- ☐
- ☐

List & score Positives

WEEK 1: WTAG SCORE

- ☐
- ☐
- ☐
- ☐

WEEK 2: WTAG SCORE

- ☐
- ☐
- ☐
- ☐

WEEK 3: WTAG SCORE

- ☐
- ☐
- ☐
- ☐

WEEK 4: WTAG SCORE

- ☐
- ☐
- ☐
- ☐

WEEK 5: WTAG SCORE

- ☐
- ☐
- ☐
- ☐

Weekly Team Member

W.T.A.G. (WORKED TOWARD ANNUAL GOAL) SCORE 1- 10 BELOW ANNUAL GOAL:

List & score opportunities

WEEK 1: WTAG SCORE

- [ ]
- [ ]
- [ ]
- [ ]

WEEK 2: WTAG SCORE

- [ ]
- [ ]
- [ ]
- [ ]

WEEK 3: WTAG SCORE

- [ ]
- [ ]
- [ ]
- [ ]

WEEK 4: WTAG SCORE

- [ ]
- [ ]
- [ ]
- [ ]

WEEK 5: WTAG SCORE

- [ ]
- [ ]
- [ ]
- [ ]

List & score Positives

WEEK 1: WTAG SCORE

- [ ]
- [ ]
- [ ]
- [ ]

WEEK 2: WTAG SCORE

- [ ]
- [ ]
- [ ]
- [ ]

WEEK 3: WTAG SCORE

- [ ]
- [ ]
- [ ]
- [ ]

WEEK 4: WTAG SCORE

- [ ]
- [ ]
- [ ]
- [ ]

WEEK 5: WTAG SCORE

- [ ]
- [ ]
- [ ]
- [ ]

WEEKLY TEAM MEMBER

W.T.A.G. (WORKED TOWARD ANNUAL GOAL) SCORE 1- 10 BELOW ANNUAL GOAL:

LIST & SCORE OPPORTUNITIES

WEEK 1: WTAG SCORE

- [ ]
- [ ]
- [ ]
- [ ]

WEEK 2: WTAG SCORE

- [ ]
- [ ]
- [ ]
- [ ]

WEEK 3: WTAG SCORE

- [ ]
- [ ]
- [ ]
- [ ]

WEEK 4: WTAG SCORE

- [ ]
- [ ]
- [ ]
- [ ]

WEEK 5: WTAG SCORE

- [ ]
- [ ]
- [ ]
- [ ]

LIST & SCORE POSITIVES

WEEK 1: WTAG SCORE

- [ ]
- [ ]
- [ ]
- [ ]

WEEK 2: WTAG SCORE

- [ ]
- [ ]
- [ ]
- [ ]

WEEK 3: WTAG SCORE

- [ ]
- [ ]
- [ ]
- [ ]

WEEK 4: WTAG SCORE

- [ ]
- [ ]
- [ ]
- [ ]

WEEK 5: WTAG SCORE

- [ ]
- [ ]
- [ ]
- [ ]

Weekly Team Member

W.T.A.G. (WORKED TOWARD ANNUAL GOAL) SCORE 1- 10 BELOW ANNUAL GOAL:

List & score opportunities

WEEK 1: WTAG SCORE

- ☐
- ☐
- ☐
- ☐

WEEK 2: WTAG SCORE

- ☐
- ☐
- ☐
- ☐

WEEK 3: WTAG SCORE

- ☐
- ☐
- ☐
- ☐

WEEK 4: WTAG SCORE

- ☐
- ☐
- ☐
- ☐

WEEK 5: WTAG SCORE

- ☐
- ☐
- ☐
- ☐

List & score Positives

WEEK 1: WTAG SCORE

- ☐
- ☐
- ☐
- ☐

WEEK 2: WTAG SCORE

- ☐
- ☐
- ☐
- ☐

WEEK 3: WTAG SCORE

- ☐
- ☐
- ☐
- ☐

WEEK 4: WTAG SCORE

- ☐
- ☐
- ☐
- ☐

WEEK 5: WTAG SCORE

- ☐
- ☐
- ☐
- ☐

Weekly Team Member

W.T.A.G. (WORKED TOWARD ANNUAL GOAL) SCORE 1- 10 BELOW ANNUAL GOAL:

List & score opportunities

WEEK 1: WTAG SCORE

- ☐
- ☐
- ☐
- ☐

WEEK 2: WTAG SCORE

- ☐
- ☐
- ☐
- ☐

WEEK 3: WTAG SCORE

- ☐
- ☐
- ☐
- ☐

WEEK 4: WTAG SCORE

- ☐
- ☐
- ☐
- ☐

WEEK 5: WTAG SCORE

- ☐
- ☐
- ☐
- ☐

List & score Positives

WEEK 1: WTAG SCORE

- ☐
- ☐
- ☐
- ☐

WEEK 2: WTAG SCORE

- ☐
- ☐
- ☐
- ☐

WEEK 3: WTAG SCORE

- ☐
- ☐
- ☐
- ☐

WEEK 4: WTAG SCORE

- ☐
- ☐
- ☐
- ☐

WEEK 5: WTAG SCORE

- ☐
- ☐
- ☐
- ☐

WEEKLY TEAM MEMBER

W.T.A.G. (WORKED TOWARD ANNUAL GOAL) SCORE 1- 10 BELOW ANNUAL GOAL:

LIST & SCORE OPPORTUNITIES

WEEK 1: WTAG SCORE

- ☐
- ☐
- ☐
- ☐

WEEK 2: WTAG SCORE

- ☐
- ☐
- ☐
- ☐

WEEK 3: WTAG SCORE

- ☐
- ☐
- ☐
- ☐

WEEK 4: WTAG SCORE

- ☐
- ☐
- ☐
- ☐

WEEK 5: WTAG SCORE

- ☐
- ☐
- ☐
- ☐

LIST & SCORE POSITIVES

WEEK 1: WTAG SCORE

- ☐
- ☐
- ☐
- ☐

WEEK 2: WTAG SCORE

- ☐
- ☐
- ☐
- ☐

WEEK 3: WTAG SCORE

- ☐
- ☐
- ☐
- ☐

WEEK 4: WTAG SCORE

- ☐
- ☐
- ☐
- ☐

WEEK 5: WTAG SCORE

- ☐
- ☐
- ☐
- ☐

Weekly Team Member

W.T.A.G. (WORKED TOWARD ANNUAL GOAL) SCORE 1- 10 BELOW ANNUAL GOAL:

List & score opportunities

WEEK 1: WTAG SCORE

- [ ]
- [ ]
- [ ]
- [ ]

WEEK 2: WTAG SCORE

- [ ]
- [ ]
- [ ]
- [ ]

WEEK 3: WTAG SCORE

- [ ]
- [ ]
- [ ]
- [ ]

WEEK 4: WTAG SCORE

- [ ]
- [ ]
- [ ]
- [ ]

WEEK 5: WTAG SCORE

- [ ]
- [ ]
- [ ]
- [ ]

List & score Positives

WEEK 1: WTAG SCORE

- [ ]
- [ ]
- [ ]
- [ ]

WEEK 2: WTAG SCORE

- [ ]
- [ ]
- [ ]
- [ ]

WEEK 3: WTAG SCORE

- [ ]
- [ ]
- [ ]
- [ ]

WEEK 4: WTAG SCORE

- [ ]
- [ ]
- [ ]
- [ ]

WEEK 5: WTAG SCORE

- [ ]
- [ ]
- [ ]
- [ ]

WEEKLY TEAM MEMBER

W.T.A.G. (WORKED TOWARD ANNUAL GOAL) SCORE 1- 10 BELOW ANNUAL GOAL:

LIST & SCORE OPPORTUNITIES

WEEK 1: WTAG SCORE

- [ ]
- [ ]
- [ ]
- [ ]

WEEK 2: WTAG SCORE

- [ ]
- [ ]
- [ ]
- [ ]

WEEK 3: WTAG SCORE

- [ ]
- [ ]
- [ ]
- [ ]

WEEK 4: WTAG SCORE

- [ ]
- [ ]
- [ ]
- [ ]

WEEK 5: WTAG SCORE

- [ ]
- [ ]
- [ ]
- [ ]

LIST & SCORE POSITIVES

WEEK 1: WTAG SCORE

- [ ]
- [ ]
- [ ]
- [ ]

WEEK 2: WTAG SCORE

- [ ]
- [ ]
- [ ]
- [ ]

WEEK 3: WTAG SCORE

- [ ]
- [ ]
- [ ]
- [ ]

WEEK 4: WTAG SCORE

- [ ]
- [ ]
- [ ]
- [ ]

WEEK 5: WTAG SCORE

- [ ]
- [ ]
- [ ]
- [ ]

Weekly Team Member

W.T.A.G. (WORKED TOWARD ANNUAL GOAL) SCORE 1- 10 BELOW ANNUAL GOAL: ____

List & Score Opportunities

WEEK 1: WTAG SCORE ____

- [ ] ____
- [ ] ____
- [ ] ____
- [ ] ____

WEEK 2: WTAG SCORE ____

- [ ] ____
- [ ] ____
- [ ] ____
- [ ] ____

WEEK 3: WTAG SCORE ____

- [ ] ____
- [ ] ____
- [ ] ____
- [ ] ____

WEEK 4: WTAG SCORE ____

- [ ] ____
- [ ] ____
- [ ] ____
- [ ] ____

WEEK 5: WTAG SCORE ____

- [ ] ____
- [ ] ____
- [ ] ____
- [ ] ____

List & Score Positives

WEEK 1: WTAG SCORE ____

- [ ] ____
- [ ] ____
- [ ] ____
- [ ] ____

WEEK 2: WTAG SCORE ____

- [ ] ____
- [ ] ____
- [ ] ____
- [ ] ____

WEEK 3: WTAG SCORE ____

- [ ] ____
- [ ] ____
- [ ] ____
- [ ] ____

WEEK 4: WTAG SCORE ____

- [ ] ____
- [ ] ____
- [ ] ____
- [ ] ____

WEEK 5: WTAG SCORE ____

- [ ] ____
- [ ] ____
- [ ] ____
- [ ] ____

Weekly Team Member

____

W.T.A.G. (WORKED TOWARD ANNUAL GOAL) SCORE 1- 10 BELOW ANNUAL GOAL: ______________

____

List & score Opportunities

WEEK 1: WTAG SCORE ______________
- ☐ ______________
- ☐ ______________
- ☐ ______________
- ☐ ______________

WEEK 2: WTAG SCORE ______________
- ☐ ______________
- ☐ ______________
- ☐ ______________
- ☐ ______________

WEEK 3: WTAG SCORE ______________
- ☐ ______________
- ☐ ______________
- ☐ ______________
- ☐ ______________

WEEK 4: WTAG SCORE ______________
- ☐ ______________
- ☐ ______________
- ☐ ______________
- ☐ ______________

WEEK 5: WTAG SCORE ______________
- ☐ ______________
- ☐ ______________
- ☐ ______________
- ☐ ______________

List & score Positives

WEEK 1: WTAG SCORE ______________
- ☐ ______________
- ☐ ______________
- ☐ ______________
- ☐ ______________

WEEK 2: WTAG SCORE ______________
- ☐ ______________
- ☐ ______________
- ☐ ______________
- ☐ ______________

WEEK 3: WTAG SCORE ______________
- ☐ ______________
- ☐ ______________
- ☐ ______________
- ☐ ______________

WEEK 4: WTAG SCORE ______________
- ☐ ______________
- ☐ ______________
- ☐ ______________
- ☐ ______________

WEEK 5: WTAG SCORE ______________
- ☐ ______________
- ☐ ______________
- ☐ ______________
- ☐ ______________

WEEKLY TEAM MEMBER

____

W.T.A.G. (WORKED TOWARD ANNUAL GOAL) SCORE 1- 10 BELOW ANNUAL GOAL: ______________

____

LIST & SCORE OPPORTUNITIES

WEEK 1: WTAG SCORE ______________

- ☐ ______________
- ☐ ______________
- ☐ ______________
- ☐ ______________

WEEK 2: WTAG SCORE ______________

- ☐ ______________
- ☐ ______________
- ☐ ______________
- ☐ ______________

WEEK 3: WTAG SCORE ______________

- ☐ ______________
- ☐ ______________
- ☐ ______________
- ☐ ______________

WEEK 4: WTAG SCORE ______________

- ☐ ______________
- ☐ ______________
- ☐ ______________
- ☐ ______________

WEEK 5: WTAG SCORE ______________

- ☐ ______________
- ☐ ______________
- ☐ ______________
- ☐ ______________

LIST & SCORE POSITIVES

WEEK 1: WTAG SCORE ______________

- ☐ ______________
- ☐ ______________
- ☐ ______________
- ☐ ______________

WEEK 2: WTAG SCORE ______________

- ☐ ______________
- ☐ ______________
- ☐ ______________
- ☐ ______________

WEEK 3: WTAG SCORE ______________

- ☐ ______________
- ☐ ______________
- ☐ ______________
- ☐ ______________

WEEK 4: WTAG SCORE ______________

- ☐ ______________
- ☐ ______________
- ☐ ______________
- ☐ ______________

WEEK 5: WTAG SCORE ______________

- ☐ ______________
- ☐ ______________
- ☐ ______________
- ☐ ______________

Weekly Team Member

W.T.A.G. (WORKED TOWARD ANNUAL GOAL) SCORE 1- 10 BELOW ANNUAL GOAL:

List & score opportunities

WEEK 1: WTAG SCORE

- ☐
- ☐
- ☐
- ☐

WEEK 2: WTAG SCORE

- ☐
- ☐
- ☐
- ☐

WEEK 3: WTAG SCORE

- ☐
- ☐
- ☐
- ☐

WEEK 4: WTAG SCORE

- ☐
- ☐
- ☐
- ☐

WEEK 5: WTAG SCORE

- ☐
- ☐
- ☐
- ☐

List & score Positives

WEEK 1: WTAG SCORE

- ☐
- ☐
- ☐
- ☐

WEEK 2: WTAG SCORE

- ☐
- ☐
- ☐
- ☐

WEEK 3: WTAG SCORE

- ☐
- ☐
- ☐
- ☐

WEEK 4: WTAG SCORE

- ☐
- ☐
- ☐
- ☐

WEEK 5: WTAG SCORE

- ☐
- ☐
- ☐
- ☐

Weekly Team Member

W.T.A.G. (WORKED TOWARD ANNUAL GOAL) SCORE 1- 10 BELOW ANNUAL GOAL:

List & score opportunities	List & score Positives
WEEK 1: WTAG SCORE	WEEK 1: WTAG SCORE
☐	☐
☐	☐
☐	☐
☐	☐
WEEK 2: WTAG SCORE	WEEK 2: WTAG SCORE
☐	☐
☐	☐
☐	☐
☐	☐
WEEK 3: WTAG SCORE	WEEK 3: WTAG SCORE
☐	☐
☐	☐
☐	☐
☐	☐
WEEK 4: WTAG SCORE	WEEK 4: WTAG SCORE
☐	☐
☐	☐
☐	☐
☐	☐
WEEK 5: WTAG SCORE	WEEK 5: WTAG SCORE
☐	☐
☐	☐
☐	☐
☐	☐

TEAM MEETING

"Success is not final, failure is not fatal: It is the courage to continue that counts." - Winston Churchill

WEEK: ____________

WINS/SUCCESSES

OPPORTUNITIES FOR IMPROVEMENT

PROJECTIONS & MONTHLY GOAL TRACKING

NEW PATIENTS: ____________

CAPTURE RATE: ____________

AVERAGE SALE: ____________

STAFF PRODUCTIVITY: ____________

WEEKLY CHECKLIST TO ACHIEVE MONTHLY GOAL

- ☐ ____________
- ☐ ____________
- ☐ ____________
- ☐ ____________

NOTES

DAILY PERSONAL PLANNER

DATE: ____________________ S M T W T F S

"Failure is simply the opportunity to begin again, this time more intelligently"
- Henry Ford.

TODAY'S SCHEDULE

6:00 ____________________

7:00 ____________________

8:00 ____________________

9:00 ____________________

10:00 ____________________

11:00 ____________________

12:00 ____________________

13:00 ____________________

14:00 ____________________

15:00 ____________________

16:00 ____________________

17:00 ____________________

18:00 ____________________

19:00 ____________________

20:00 ____________________

21:00 ____________________

22:00 ____________________

ACTION PLAN (TOP 3 PRIORITIES)

- ☐ ____________________
- ☐ ____________________
- ☐ ____________________

TASKS

- ☐ ____________________
- ☐ ____________________
- ☐ ____________________

WORK OUT COMPLETE

- ☐

WATER INTAKE

BREAKFAST PLAN ____________________

LUNCH PLAN ____________________

DINNER PLAN ____________________

HOURS SLEPT ____________________

END OF DAY REFLECTION: CELEBRATE TEAM MEMBERS & DAILY SUCCESS

____

____

END OF DAY REFLECTION: WHAT NEEDS IMPROVEMENT?

____

____

Daily Personal Planner

DATE: ____________________ S M T W T F S

"Your most unhappy patient is your greatest source of learning"
- Bill Gates

Today's Schedule

6:00

7:00

8:00

9:00

10:00

11:00

12:00

13:00

14:00

15:00

16:00

17:00

18:00

19:00

20:00

21:00

22:00

Action Plan (Top 3 priorities)

- [ ]
- [ ]
- [ ]

TASKS

- [ ]
- [ ]
- [ ]

WORK OUT COMPLETE

- [ ]

WATER INTAKE

Breakfast Plan ____________________

Lunch Plan ____________________

Dinner Plan ____________________

Hours Slept ____________________

End of Day Reflection: Celebrate Team members & Daily success

End of Day Reflection: what needs improvement?

DAILY PERSONAL PLANNER

DATE: ____________________ S M T W T F S

"The way to get started is to quit talking and begin doing."
- Walt Disney

TODAY'S SCHEDULE

6:00
7:00
8:00
9:00
10:00
11:00
12:00
13:00
14:00
15:00
16:00
17:00
18:00
19:00
20:00
21:00
22:00

ACTION PLAN (TOP 3 PRIORITIES)

- ☐
- ☐
- ☐

TASKS

- ☐
- ☐
- ☐

WORK OUT COMPLETE

- ☐

WATER INTAKE

BREAKFAST PLAN

LUNCH PLAN

DINNER PLAN

HOURS SLEPT

END OF DAY REFLECTION: CELEBRATE TEAM MEMBERS & DAILY SUCCESS

END OF DAY REFLECTION: WHAT NEEDS IMPROVEMENT?

Daily Personal Planner

DATE: ____________________ S M T W T F S

"Whether you think you can or you can't, you're right"
- Henry Ford

Today's Schedule

6:00 ______
7:00 ______
8:00 ______
9:00 ______
10:00 ______
11:00 ______
12:00 ______
13:00 ______
14:00 ______
15:00 ______
16:00 ______
17:00 ______
18:00 ______
19:00 ______
20:00 ______
21:00 ______
22:00 ______

Action Plan (Top 3 priorities)

☐ ______
☐ ______
☐ ______

Tasks

☐ ______
☐ ______
☐ ______

Work Out Complete

☐

Water Intake

Breakfast Plan ______

Lunch Plan ______

Dinner Plan ______

Hours Slept ______

End of Day Reflection: Celebrate Team members & Daily success

______
______

End of Day Reflection: what needs improvement?

______
______

Daily Personal Planner

DATE: ______________________ S M T W T F S

Innovation distinguishes between a leader and a follower"
- Steve Jobs

Today's Schedule

6:00
7:00
8:00
9:00
10:00
11:00
12:00
13:00
14:00
15:00
16:00
17:00
18:00
19:00
20:00
21:00
22:00

Action Plan (Top 3 priorities)

- ☐
- ☐
- ☐

TASKS

- ☐
- ☐
- ☐

WORK OUT COMPLETE

- ☐

WATER INTAKE

Breakfast Plan

Lunch Plan

Dinner Plan

Hours Slept

End of Day Reflection: Celebrate Team members & Daily success

End of Day Reflection: what needs improvement?

Daily Personal Planner

DATE: ______________ S M T W T F S

"Successful entrepreneurs are lifelong learners who are constantly looking for ways to improve and grow".
- Unknown

Today's Schedule

6:00 ______
7:00 ______
8:00 ______
9:00 ______
10:00 ______
11:00 ______
12:00 ______
13:00 ______
14:00 ______
15:00 ______
16:00 ______
17:00 ______
18:00 ______
19:00 ______
20:00 ______
21:00 ______
22:00 ______

Action Plan (Top 3 priorities)

- [ ] ______
- [ ] ______
- [ ] ______

TASKS

- [ ] ______
- [ ] ______
- [ ] ______

WORK OUT COMPLETE

- [ ]

WATER INTAKE

Breakfast Plan ______

Lunch Plan ______

Dinner Plan ______

Hours Slept ______

End of Day Reflection: Celebrate Team members & Daily success

______

______

End of Day Reflection: what needs improvement?

______

______

DAILY PERSONAL PLANNER

DATE: ____________ S M T W T F S

"Successful entrepreneurs don't wait for opportunities; they create them"
- Unknown

TODAY'S SCHEDULE

6:00
7:00
8:00
9:00
10:00
11:00
12:00
13:00
14:00
15:00
16:00
17:00
18:00
19:00
20:00
21:00
22:00

ACTION PLAN (TOP 3 PRIORITIES)

- ☐
- ☐
- ☐

TASKS

- ☐
- ☐
- ☐

WORK OUT COMPLETE

- ☐

WATER INTAKE

BREAKFAST PLAN ____________

LUNCH PLAN ____________

DINNER PLAN ____________

HOURS SLEPT ____________

END OF DAY REFLECTION: CELEBRATE TEAM MEMBERS & DAILY SUCCESS

END OF DAY REFLECTION: WHAT NEEDS IMPROVEMENT?

Team Meeting

Week: ____________

WINS/SUCCESSES

OPPORTUNITIES FOR IMPROVEMENT

Projections & Monthly Goal Tracking

New Patients: ____________

Capture Rate: ____________

Average Sale: ____________

Staff Productivity: ____________

Weekly Checklist to Achieve Monthly Goal

- [ ] ____________
- [ ] ____________
- [ ] ____________
- [ ] ____________

Notes

Daily Personal Planner

Date: ____________________   S M T W T F S

"A successful business is built on passion and hard work"
- Unknown

Today's Schedule

6:00 ____________________
7:00 ____________________
8:00 ____________________
9:00 ____________________
10:00 ____________________
11:00 ____________________
12:00 ____________________
13:00 ____________________
14:00 ____________________
15:00 ____________________
16:00 ____________________
17:00 ____________________
18:00 ____________________
19:00 ____________________
20:00 ____________________
21:00 ____________________
22:00 ____________________

Action Plan (Top 3 priorities)

- ☐ ____________________
- ☐ ____________________
- ☐ ____________________

Tasks

- ☐ ____________________
- ☐ ____________________
- ☐ ____________________

Work out complete

- ☐

Water intake

Breakfast Plan ____________________

Lunch Plan ____________________

Dinner Plan ____________________

Hours Slept ____________________

End of Day Reflection: Celebrate Team members & Daily success

____

____

End of Day Reflection: what needs improvement?

____

____

Daily Personal Planner

DATE: ____________________ S M T W T F S

"It does not matter how slowly you go so long as you do not stop"
- Confucious

Today's Schedule

6:00
7:00
8:00
9:00
10:00
11:00
12:00
13:00
14:00
15:00
16:00
17:00
18:00
19:00
20:00
21:00
22:00

Action Plan (Top 3 priorities)

- ☐
- ☐
- ☐

TASKS

- ☐
- ☐
- ☐

WORK OUT COMPLETE

- ☐

WATER INTAKE

Breakfast Plan ____________________

Lunch Plan ____________________

Dinner Plan ____________________

Hours Slept ____________________

End of Day Reflection: Celebrate Team members & Daily success

End of Day Reflection: what needs improvement?

DAILY PERSONAL PLANNER

DATE: ____________________ S M T W T F S

"There are no secrets to success. It is the result of preparation, hard work, and learning from failure"
- Colin Powell

TODAY'S SCHEDULE

6:00
7:00
8:00
9:00
10:00
11:00
12:00
13:00
14:00
15:00
16:00
17:00
18:00
19:00
20:00
21:00
22:00

ACTION PLAN (TOP 3 PRIORITIES)

- ☐
- ☐
- ☐

TASKS

- ☐
- ☐
- ☐

WORK OUT COMPLETE

☐

WATER INTAKE

BREAKFAST PLAN ____________________

LUNCH PLAN ____________________

DINNER PLAN ____________________

HOURS SLEPT ____________________

END OF DAY REFLECTION: CELEBRATE TEAM MEMBERS & DAILY SUCCESS

END OF DAY REFLECTION: WHAT NEEDS IMPROVEMENT?

DAILY PERSONAL PLANNER

DATE: ______________________ S M T W T F S

"The best way to predict the future is to create it."
- Abraham Lincoln

TODAY'S SCHEDULE

6:00
7:00
8:00
9:00
10:00
11:00
12:00
13:00
14:00
15:00
16:00
17:00
18:00
19:00
20:00
21:00
22:00

ACTION PLAN (TOP 3 PRIORITIES)

- ☐
- ☐
- ☐

TASKS

- ☐
- ☐
- ☐

WORK OUT COMPLETE

☐

WATER INTAKE

BREAKFAST PLAN

LUNCH PLAN

DINNER PLAN

HOURS SLEPT

END OF DAY REFLECTION: CELEBRATE TEAM MEMBERS & DAILY SUCCESS

END OF DAY REFLECTION: WHAT NEEDS IMPROVEMENT?

Daily Personal Planner

DATE: ____________________ S M T W T F S

"Your work is going to fill a large part of your life, and the only way to be truly satisfied is to do what you believe is great work. And the only way to do great work is to love what you do." - Steve Jobs

TODAY'S SCHEDULE

6:00

7:00

8:00

9:00

10:00

11:00

12:00

13:00

14:00

15:00

16:00

17:00

18:00

19:00

20:00

21:00

22:00

ACTION PLAN (TOP 3 PRIORITIES)

- ☐
- ☐
- ☐

TASKS

- ☐
- ☐
- ☐

WORK OUT COMPLETE

☐

WATER INTAKE

BREAKFAST PLAN

LUNCH PLAN

DINNER PLAN

HOURS SLEPT

END OF DAY REFLECTION: CELEBRATE TEAM MEMBERS & DAILY SUCCESS

END OF DAY REFLECTION: WHAT NEEDS IMPROVEMENT?

Daily Personal Planner

DATE: ________________ S M T W T F S

"Don't wait for opportunities, create them."
- Charles R. Schwab

TODAY'S SCHEDULE

6:00
7:00
8:00
9:00
10:00
11:00
12:00
13:00
14:00
15:00
16:00
17:00
18:00
19:00
20:00
21:00
22:00

ACTION PLAN (TOP 3 PRIORITIES)

- ▢
- ▢
- ▢

TASKS

- ▢
- ▢
- ▢

WORK OUT COMPLETE

▢

WATER INTAKE

BREAKFAST PLAN ________________

LUNCH PLAN ________________

DINNER PLAN ________________

HOURS SLEPT ________________

END OF DAY REFLECTION: CELEBRATE TEAM MEMBERS & DAILY SUCCESS

END OF DAY REFLECTION: WHAT NEEDS IMPROVEMENT?

DAILY PERSONAL PLANNER

DATE: ______________________ S M T W T F S

"The biggest risk is not taking any risk. In a world that's changing quickly, the only strategy that is guaranteed to fail is not taking risks." - Mark Zuckerberg

TODAY'S SCHEDULE

6:00

7:00

8:00

9:00

10:00

11:00

12:00

13:00

14:00

15:00

16:00

17:00

18:00

19:00

20:00

21:00

22:00

ACTION PLAN (TOP 3 PRIORITIES)

- ▢
- ▢
- ▢

TASKS

- ▢
- ▢
- ▢

WORK OUT COMPLETE

▢

WATER INTAKE

BREAKFAST PLAN

LUNCH PLAN

DINNER PLAN

HOURS SLEPT

END OF DAY REFLECTION: CELEBRATE TEAM MEMBERS & DAILY SUCCESS

END OF DAY REFLECTION: WHAT NEEDS IMPROVEMENT?

TEAM MEETING

WEEK: ____________

WINS/SUCCESSES

OPPORTUNITIES FOR IMPROVEMENT

PROJECTIONS & MONTHLY GOAL TRACKING

NEW PATIENTS: ____________

CAPTURE RATE: ____________

AVERAGE SALE: ____________

STAFF PRODUCTIVITY: ____________

WEEKLY CHECKLIST TO ACHIEVE MONTHLY GOAL

- ☐ ____________
- ☐ ____________
- ☐ ____________
- ☐ ____________

NOTES

Daily Personal Planner

Date: ____________________ S M T W T F S

"The biggest adventure you can ever take is to live the life of your dreams."
- Oprah Winfrey

Today's Schedule

6:00 ____________________
7:00 ____________________
8:00 ____________________
9:00 ____________________
10:00 ____________________
11:00 ____________________
12:00 ____________________
13:00 ____________________
14:00 ____________________
15:00 ____________________
16:00 ____________________
17:00 ____________________
18:00 ____________________
19:00 ____________________
20:00 ____________________
21:00 ____________________
22:00 ____________________

Action Plan (Top 3 priorities)

- ☐ ____________________
- ☐ ____________________
- ☐ ____________________

Tasks

- ☐ ____________________
- ☐ ____________________
- ☐ ____________________

Work out complete

- ☐

Water intake

Breakfast Plan ____________________

Lunch Plan ____________________

Dinner Plan ____________________

Hours Slept ____________________

End of Day Reflection: Celebrate Team members & Daily success

____

____

End of Day Reflection: what needs improvement?

____

____

DAILY PERSONAL PLANNER

DATE: ______________________ S M T W T F S

"Success is not the key to happiness. Happiness is the key to success. If you love what you are doing, you will be successful." - Albert Schweitzer

TODAY'S SCHEDULE

6:00

7:00

8:00

9:00

10:00

11:00

12:00

13:00

14:00

15:00

16:00

17:00

18:00

19:00

20:00

21:00

22:00

ACTION PLAN (TOP 3 PRIORITIES)

- ☐
- ☐
- ☐

TASKS

- ☐
- ☐
- ☐

WORK OUT COMPLETE

☐

WATER INTAKE

BREAKFAST PLAN

LUNCH PLAN

DINNER PLAN

HOURS SLEPT

END OF DAY REFLECTION: CELEBRATE TEAM MEMBERS & DAILY SUCCESS

END OF DAY REFLECTION: WHAT NEEDS IMPROVEMENT?

DAILY PERSONAL PLANNER

DATE: ____________________ S M T W T F S

"The only limit to our realization of tomorrow will be our doubts of today."
- Franklin D. Roosevelt

TODAY'S SCHEDULE

6:00
7:00
8:00
9:00
10:00
11:00
12:00
13:00
14:00
15:00
16:00
17:00
18:00
19:00
20:00
21:00
22:00

ACTION PLAN (TOP 3 PRIORITIES)

- ▢
- ▢
- ▢

TASKS

- ▢
- ▢
- ▢

WORK OUT COMPLETE

▢

WATER INTAKE

BREAKFAST PLAN ____________________

LUNCH PLAN ____________________

DINNER PLAN ____________________

HOURS SLEPT ____________________

END OF DAY REFLECTION: CELEBRATE TEAM MEMBERS & DAILY SUCCESS

END OF DAY REFLECTION: WHAT NEEDS IMPROVEMENT?

Daily Personal Planner

DATE: ______________________ S M T W T F S

"You miss 100% of the shots you don't take."
- Wayne Gretzky

Today's Schedule

6:00 ______
7:00 ______
8:00 ______
9:00 ______
10:00 ______
11:00 ______
12:00 ______
13:00 ______
14:00 ______
15:00 ______
16:00 ______
17:00 ______
18:00 ______
19:00 ______
20:00 ______
21:00 ______
22:00 ______

Action Plan (Top 3 priorities)

- [ ] ______
- [ ] ______
- [ ] ______

TASKS

- [ ] ______
- [ ] ______
- [ ] ______

WORK OUT COMPLETE

- [ ]

WATER INTAKE

Breakfast Plan ______

Lunch Plan ______

Dinner Plan ______

Hours Slept ______

End of Day Reflection: Celebrate Team members & Daily success

______

______

End of Day Reflection: what needs improvement?

______

______

Daily Personal Planner

Date: ______________________ S M T W T F S

"The best way to find yourself is to lose yourself in the service of others."
- Mahatma Gandhi

Today's Schedule

6:00 ____________________

7:00 ____________________

8:00 ____________________

9:00 ____________________

10:00 ____________________

11:00 ____________________

12:00 ____________________

13:00 ____________________

14:00 ____________________

15:00 ____________________

16:00 ____________________

17:00 ____________________

18:00 ____________________

19:00 ____________________

20:00 ____________________

21:00 ____________________

22:00 ____________________

Action Plan (Top 3 priorities)

- [ ] ____________________
- [ ] ____________________
- [ ] ____________________

TASKS

- [ ] ____________________
- [ ] ____________________
- [ ] ____________________

WORK OUT COMPLETE

- [ ]

WATER INTAKE

Breakfast Plan ____________________

Lunch Plan ____________________

Dinner Plan ____________________

Hours Slept ____________________

End of Day Reflection: Celebrate Team members & Daily success

____

____

End of Day Reflection: what needs improvement?

____

____

DAILY PERSONAL PLANNER

DATE: ______________________ S M T W T F S

"The only way to do great work is to love what you do. If you haven't found it yet, keep looking. Don't settle. As with all matters of the heart, you'll know when you find it."
- Steve Jobs

TODAY'S SCHEDULE

6:00 ____________________
7:00 ____________________
8:00 ____________________
9:00 ____________________
10:00 ____________________
11:00 ____________________
12:00 ____________________
13:00 ____________________
14:00 ____________________
15:00 ____________________
16:00 ____________________
17:00 ____________________
18:00 ____________________
19:00 ____________________
20:00 ____________________
21:00 ____________________
22:00 ____________________

ACTION PLAN (TOP 3 PRIORITIES)

- [ ] ____________________
- [ ] ____________________
- [ ] ____________________

TASKS

- [ ] ____________________
- [ ] ____________________
- [ ] ____________________

WORK OUT COMPLETE

- [ ]

WATER INTAKE

BREAKFAST PLAN ____________________

LUNCH PLAN ____________________

DINNER PLAN ____________________

HOURS SLEPT ____________________

END OF DAY REFLECTION: CELEBRATE TEAM MEMBERS & DAILY SUCCESS

____

____

END OF DAY REFLECTION: WHAT NEEDS IMPROVEMENT?

____

____

DAILY PERSONAL PLANNER

DATE: ____________ S M T W T F S

"The best time to plant a tree was 20 years ago. The second best time is now."
- Chinese Proverb

TODAY'S SCHEDULE

6:00 ____________
7:00 ____________
8:00 ____________
9:00 ____________
10:00 ____________
11:00 ____________
12:00 ____________
13:00 ____________
14:00 ____________
15:00 ____________
16:00 ____________
17:00 ____________
18:00 ____________
19:00 ____________
20:00 ____________
21:00 ____________
22:00 ____________

ACTION PLAN (TOP 3 PRIORITIES)

- ☐ ____________
- ☐ ____________
- ☐ ____________

TASKS

- ☐ ____________
- ☐ ____________
- ☐ ____________

WORK OUT COMPLETE

- ☐

WATER INTAKE

BREAKFAST PLAN ____________

LUNCH PLAN ____________

DINNER PLAN ____________

HOURS SLEPT ____________

END OF DAY REFLECTION: CELEBRATE TEAM MEMBERS & DAILY SUCCESS

____

____

END OF DAY REFLECTION: WHAT NEEDS IMPROVEMENT?

____

____

TEAM MEETING

WEEK: ____________

WINS/SUCCESSES

OPPORTUNITIES FOR IMPROVEMENT

PROJECTIONS & MONTHLY GOAL TRACKING

NEW PATIENTS: ____________

CAPTURE RATE: ____________

AVERAGE SALE: ____________

STAFF PRODUCTIVITY: ____________

WEEKLY CHECKLIST TO ACHIEVE MONTHLY GOAL

- ☐ ____________
- ☐ ____________
- ☐ ____________
- ☐ ____________

NOTES

Daily Personal Planner

DATE: ____________________ S M T W T F S

• "You can't build a reputation on what you are going to do."
- Henry Ford

Today's Schedule

6:00 ____
7:00 ____
8:00 ____
9:00 ____
10:00 ____
11:00 ____
12:00 ____
13:00 ____
14:00 ____
15:00 ____
16:00 ____
17:00 ____
18:00 ____
19:00 ____
20:00 ____
21:00 ____
22:00 ____

Action Plan (Top 3 priorities)

- ☐ ____
- ☐ ____
- ☐ ____

TASKS

- ☐ ____
- ☐ ____
- ☐ ____

WORK OUT COMPLETE

☐

WATER INTAKE

Breakfast Plan ____

Lunch Plan ____

Dinner Plan ____

Hours Slept ____

End of Day Reflection: Celebrate Team members & Daily success

____

____

End of Day Reflection: What needs improvement?

____

____

Daily Personal Planner

Date: ____________________ S M T W T F S

"Your most unhappy patient is your greatest source of learning"
- Bill Gates

Today's Schedule

6:00

7:00

8:00

9:00

10:00

11:00

12:00

13:00

14:00

15:00

16:00

17:00

18:00

19:00

20:00

21:00

22:00

Action Plan (Top 3 priorities)

- ☐
- ☐
- ☐

TASKS

- ☐
- ☐
- ☐

WORK OUT COMPLETE

☐

WATER INTAKE

Breakfast Plan ____________________

Lunch Plan ____________________

Dinner Plan ____________________

Hours Slept ____________________

End of Day Reflection: Celebrate Team members & Daily success

End of Day Reflection: what needs improvement?

Daily Personal Planner

DATE: ______________________ S M T W T F S

"Success is not final, failure is not fatal: It is the courage to continue that counts."
- Winston Churchill

Today's Schedule

6:00

7:00

8:00

9:00

10:00

11:00

12:00

13:00

14:00

15:00

16:00

17:00

18:00

19:00

20:00

21:00

22:00

Action Plan (Top 3 priorities)

- ☐
- ☐
- ☐

TASKS

- ☐
- ☐
- ☐

WORK OUT COMPLETE

- ☐

WATER INTAKE

Breakfast Plan ______________________

Lunch Plan ______________________

Dinner Plan ______________________

Hours Slept ______________________

End of Day Reflection: Celebrate Team members & Daily success

End of Day Reflection: what needs improvement?

DAILY PERSONAL PLANNER

DATE: ______________________ S M T W T F S

• *"The road to success and greatness is always paved with consistent hard work. Outwork your competitors and be relentless." – Unknown*

TODAY'S SCHEDULE

6:00 ______

7:00 ______

8:00 ______

9:00 ______

10:00 ______

11:00 ______

12:00 ______

13:00 ______

14:00 ______

15:00 ______

16:00 ______

17:00 ______

18:00 ______

19:00 ______

20:00 ______

21:00 ______

22:00 ______

ACTION PLAN (TOP 3 PRIORITIES)

- ☐ ______
- ☐ ______
- ☐ ______

TASKS

- ☐ ______
- ☐ ______
- ☐ ______

WORK OUT COMPLETE

☐

WATER INTAKE

BREAKFAST PLAN ______

LUNCH PLAN ______

DINNER PLAN ______

HOURS SLEPT ______

END OF DAY REFLECTION: CELEBRATE TEAM MEMBERS & DAILY SUCCESS

______

______

END OF DAY REFLECTION: WHAT NEEDS IMPROVEMENT?

______

______

Daily Personal Planner

DATE: ____________________ S M T W T F S

"Successful people do what unsuccessful people are not willing to do. Don't wish it were easier, wish you were better." – Jim Rohn

Today's Schedule

6:00

7:00

8:00

9:00

10:00

11:00

12:00

13:00

14:00

15:00

16:00

17:00

18:00

19:00

20:00

21:00

22:00

Action Plan (Top 3 priorities)

- ☐
- ☐
- ☐

TASKS

- ☐
- ☐
- ☐

WORK OUT COMPLETE

- ☐

WATER INTAKE

Breakfast Plan ____________________

Lunch Plan ____________________

Dinner Plan ____________________

Hours Slept ____________________

End of Day Reflection: Celebrate Team members & Daily success

End of Day Reflection: what needs improvement?

Daily Personal Planner

Date: ______________ S M T W T F S

• "The best way to predict the future is to create it."
–Peter Drucker

Today's Schedule

6:00

7:00

8:00

9:00

10:00

11:00

12:00

13:00

14:00

15:00

16:00

17:00

18:00

19:00

20:00

21:00

22:00

Action Plan (Top 3 priorities)

- ☐
- ☐
- ☐

Tasks

- ☐
- ☐
- ☐

Work Out Complete

- ☐

Water Intake

Breakfast Plan ______________

Lunch Plan ______________

Dinner Plan ______________

Hours Slept ______________

End of Day Reflection: Celebrate Team members & Daily success

End of Day Reflection: What needs improvement?

DAILY PERSONAL PLANNER

DATE: ____________________ S M T W T F S

"You don't have to be great to start, but you have to start to be great."
–Zig Ziglar

TODAY'S SCHEDULE

6:00

7:00

8:00

9:00

10:00

11:00

12:00

13:00

14:00

15:00

16:00

17:00

18:00

19:00

20:00

21:00

22:00

ACTION PLAN (TOP 3 PRIORITIES)

- ☐
- ☐
- ☐

TASKS

- ☐
- ☐
- ☐

WORK OUT COMPLETE

- ☐

WATER INTAKE

BREAKFAST PLAN

LUNCH PLAN

DINNER PLAN

HOURS SLEPT

END OF DAY REFLECTION: CELEBRATE TEAM MEMBERS & DAILY SUCCESS

END OF DAY REFLECTION: WHAT NEEDS IMPROVEMENT?

Team Meeting

Week: ____________

WINS/SUCCESSES

OPPORTUNITIES FOR IMPROVEMENT

____
____
____
____
____

Projections & Monthly Goal Tracking

New Patients: ____________________

Capture Rate: ____________________

Average Sale: ____________________

Staff Productivity: ____________________

Weekly Checklist to Achieve Monthly Goal

- ☐ ______________________________
- ☐ ______________________________
- ☐ ______________________________
- ☐ ______________________________

Notes

____
____
____
____

Daily Personal Planner

DATE: ____________________ S M T W T F S

"Success is walking from failure to failure with no loss of enthusiasm."
– Winston Churchill

Today's Schedule

6:00 ____________________
7:00 ____________________
8:00 ____________________
9:00 ____________________
10:00 ____________________
11:00 ____________________
12:00 ____________________
13:00 ____________________
14:00 ____________________
15:00 ____________________
16:00 ____________________
17:00 ____________________
18:00 ____________________
19:00 ____________________
20:00 ____________________
21:00 ____________________
22:00 ____________________

Action Plan (Top 3 priorities)

- ☐ ____________________
- ☐ ____________________
- ☐ ____________________

TASKS

- ☐ ____________________
- ☐ ____________________
- ☐ ____________________

WORK OUT COMPLETE

- ☐

WATER INTAKE

Breakfast Plan ____________________

Lunch Plan ____________________

Dinner Plan ____________________

Hours Slept ____________________

End of Day Reflection: Celebrate Team members & Daily success

____

____

End of Day Reflection: what needs improvement?

____

____

DAILY PERSONAL PLANNER

DATE: ____________________ S M T W T F S

"Don't be afraid to give up the good to go for the great."
–John D. Rockefeller

TODAY'S SCHEDULE

6:00 ____
7:00 ____
8:00 ____
9:00 ____
10:00 ____
11:00 ____
12:00 ____
13:00 ____
14:00 ____
15:00 ____
16:00 ____
17:00 ____
18:00 ____
19:00 ____
20:00 ____
21:00 ____
22:00 ____

ACTION PLAN (TOP 3 PRIORITIES)

- ☐ ____
- ☐ ____
- ☐ ____

TASKS

- ☐ ____
- ☐ ____
- ☐ ____

WORK OUT COMPLETE

☐

WATER INTAKE

BREAKFAST PLAN ____

LUNCH PLAN ____

DINNER PLAN ____

HOURS SLEPT ____

END OF DAY REFLECTION: CELEBRATE TEAM MEMBERS & DAILY SUCCESS

____

____

END OF DAY REFLECTION: WHAT NEEDS IMPROVEMENT?

____

____

DAILY PERSONAL PLANNER

DATE: ____________ S M T W T F S

"Success is not the key to happiness. Happiness is the key to success. If you love what you are doing, you will be successful." – Albert Schweitzer

TODAY'S SCHEDULE

6:00

7:00

8:00

9:00

10:00

11:00

12:00

13:00

14:00

15:00

16:00

17:00

18:00

19:00

20:00

21:00

22:00

ACTION PLAN (TOP 3 PRIORITIES)

- ▢
- ▢
- ▢

TASKS

- ▢
- ▢
- ▢

WORK OUT COMPLETE

▢

WATER INTAKE

BREAKFAST PLAN ____________

LUNCH PLAN ____________

DINNER PLAN ____________

HOURS SLEPT ____________

END OF DAY REFLECTION: CELEBRATE TEAM MEMBERS & DAILY SUCCESS

END OF DAY REFLECTION: WHAT NEEDS IMPROVEMENT?

DAILY PERSONAL PLANNER

DATE: ____________________ S M T W T F S

"The most difficult thing is the decision to act, the rest is merely tenacity."
–Amelia Earhart

TODAY'S SCHEDULE

6:00
7:00
8:00
9:00
10:00
11:00
12:00
13:00
14:00
15:00
16:00
17:00
18:00
19:00
20:00
21:00
22:00

ACTION PLAN (TOP 3 PRIORITIES)

- ☐
- ☐
- ☐

TASKS

- ☐
- ☐
- ☐

WORK OUT COMPLETE

☐

WATER INTAKE

BREAKFAST PLAN

LUNCH PLAN

DINNER PLAN

HOURS SLEPT

END OF DAY REFLECTION: CELEBRATE TEAM MEMBERS & DAILY SUCCESS

END OF DAY REFLECTION: WHAT NEEDS IMPROVEMENT?

Daily Personal Planner

DATE: ______________________ S M T W T F S

"If you do what you've always done, you'll get what you've always gotten."
— Tony Robbins

Today's Schedule

6:00
7:00
8:00
9:00
10:00
11:00
12:00
13:00
14:00
15:00
16:00
17:00
18:00
19:00
20:00
21:00
22:00

Action Plan (Top 3 priorities)

- ☐
- ☐
- ☐

TASKS

- ☐
- ☐
- ☐

WORK OUT COMPLETE

- ☐

WATER INTAKE

Breakfast Plan

Lunch Plan

Dinner Plan

Hours Slept

End of Day Reflection: Celebrate Team members & Daily success

End of Day Reflection: what needs improvement?

DAILY PERSONAL PLANNER

DATE: ____________________ S M T W T F S

"Be undeniably good. No marketing effort or social media buzzword can be a substitute for that." — Anthony Volodkin

TODAY'S SCHEDULE

6:00 ____

7:00 ____

8:00 ____

9:00 ____

10:00 ____

11:00 ____

12:00 ____

13:00 ____

14:00 ____

15:00 ____

16:00 ____

17:00 ____

18:00 ____

19:00 ____

20:00 ____

21:00 ____

22:00 ____

ACTION PLAN (TOP 3 PRIORITIES)

- ☐ ____
- ☐ ____
- ☐ ____

TASKS

- ☐ ____
- ☐ ____
- ☐ ____

WORK OUT COMPLETE

☐

WATER INTAKE

BREAKFAST PLAN ____

LUNCH PLAN ____

DINNER PLAN ____

HOURS SLEPT ____

END OF DAY REFLECTION: CELEBRATE TEAM MEMBERS & DAILY SUCCESS

____

____

END OF DAY REFLECTION: WHAT NEEDS IMPROVEMENT?

____

____

Daily Personal Planner

Date: ______________ S M T W T F S

"You don't learn to walk by following rules. You learn by doing and falling over."
— Richard Branson

Today's Schedule

6:00

7:00

8:00

9:00

10:00

11:00

12:00

13:00

14:00

15:00

16:00

17:00

18:00

19:00

20:00

21:00

22:00

Action Plan (Top 3 priorities)

- ☐
- ☐
- ☐

Tasks

- ☐
- ☐
- ☐

Work out complete

- ☐

Water intake

Breakfast Plan

Lunch Plan

Dinner Plan

Hours Slept

End of Day Reflection: Celebrate Team members & Daily success

End of Day Reflection: what needs improvement?

In the

VISION ACES ACADEMY

We teach systems that will build your practice.

WHAT IF

You could increase growth through better systems? Help more patients? Increase profits? Have lots of support and individual coaching to get you there?

STEP INTO YOUR OVT PRACTICE WITH CONFIDENCE & SUCCESS!

SEE IF ANY OF THESE RESONATE WITH YOU...

Practice Owners Who Are Worn Out: You've given so much to your practice and patients, but you're not seeing your practice grow.

Those Wondering If Their Practice Can Truly Thrive: You have a full schedule but your practice is still in the red or barely breaking even.

Your Clinic Is Doing Well And You're Ready To Take It To The Next Level: You see how well your business is running, but you're convinced there have to be better and more efficient ways to increase your numbers even further.

VTODs Who Started Out With Optimism But Are Now Losing Steam: You've been at this for a few years now but your energy and hope are wavering.

You Find Staff Management Is Holding You Back: Your examinations are cutting-edge but you see things in the back office slipping: Billing, Processing of Orders, Patient Flow and Follow Up, Scheduling.

You've Reached Your Leadership Limit: It's time to focus on the big picture with your team and office. You've spent months or years focusing on patient results and now see that you need to step up your leadership and management practices.

You Know You Need Help But Don't Know Who To Trust: You've tried to get help and have spent loads of money for products and support that haven't panned out. You are looking for a reputable program to take your Vision Therapy practice to it's highest level.

Made in the USA
Monee, IL
12 November 2026

c4f73303-a8f6-4a88-96a3-b7f4b5144573R01